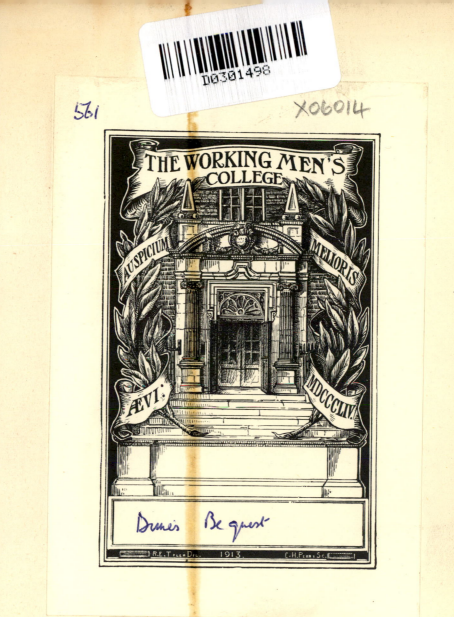

THE WORKING MEN'S COLLEGE

AUSPICIUM MELIORIS

AEVI; MDCCCLIV.

Drames Bequest

R.E.Tyler Del. 1913. C.H.Perry Sc.

ENGLISH PLACE-NAME SOCIETY. VOLUME XXII
FOR 1944–45

GENERAL EDITOR
BRUCE DICKINS

THE PLACE-NAMES OF CUMBERLAND

PART III

THE PLACE-NAMES OF CUMBERLAND

By

A. M. ARMSTRONG, A. MAWER, F. M. STENTON & BRUCE DICKINS

PART III

INTRODUCTION, ETC.

CAMBRIDGE

AT THE UNIVERSITY PRESS

1952

PUBLISHED BY
THE SYNDICS OF THE CAMBRIDGE UNIVERSITY PRESS
London Office: Bentley House, N.W. I
American Branch: New York

Agents for Canada, India, and Pakistan: Macmillan

Printed in Great Britain at the University Press, Cambridge
(Brooke Crutchley, University Printer)

PREFACE

THE major names of Cumberland have been treated by W. J. Sedgefield whose book covers Westmorland too—a precedent that might well have been followed—and by E. Ekwall in his invaluable *Dictionary of English Place-Names*. The Society's three volumes, of which this is the last to appear, have gone into greater detail, including a vast number of minor names obsolete and current. Many field-names of interest are now included in the index, as reviewers of earlier volumes in the series have repeatedly asked should be done. Whether it will be economically possible to make this the rule remains to be seen. There are also given a relief map of a new type and a reproduction of the Gospatric writ, a puzzling document of the highest interest to Cumberland antiquaries.

The place-names of Cumberland have presented problems greater than those which have faced us in previous volumes in the series, not only because of the inherent difficulties presented by the names themselves, but also because the material from which early forms can be obtained is scanty, and in many cases is preserved only in late and often unreliable copies. Only one pre-Conquest document is known to exist, and that in a late copy. For no more than four names (Bootle, Kirksanton, Whicham and the lost *Hougenai* 414–15), all in the extreme south of the county, are there Domesday forms. The cartularies of some monastic houses outside the county have provided forms of great value. The cartularies of houses in Cumberland itself, while they provide for many names our only early forms, must be treated with caution, since most of them have survived only in late copies, and it is obvious that the forms of place-names have frequently been wrongly copied. The cartularies of some of the monastic houses appear not to have survived at all. In an unusually large measure we are therefore dependent in this county on such records as the Pipe Rolls, the Assize Rolls, the Pleas of the Forest and the Feet of Fines. Such sixteenth- and seventeenth-century sources as the Land Revenue Miscellaneous Books, the Augmentation Office Miscellaneous Books and the Parliamentary Surveys have given late, but very useful forms. From documents in private hands we have got much valuable material, and our indebtedness to those who have given us access to these is expressed below. In particular the muniment rooms at Lowther Castle, at Cockermouth Castle (where the great Elizabethan survey of the Cumberland lands of the earls of Northumberland proved a rich source of forms for minor names) and at Boothby, and those of the Bishop of Carlisle and the Dean and Chapter of Carlisle, provided us with many early forms. But in some places where early documents relating to the county might have been expected, the results were disappointing, and it is clear that many documents have been destroyed, not only owing to the troubled state of this part of the country in medieval and early modern times, but in some cases because of carelessness, or lack of appreciation of their value, within the last hundred years.

The collection of the forms, alike from printed and unprinted sources, their identification, and the arrangement of the material in the volumes was nearly all done by Miss Aileen M. Armstrong. Sir Allen Mawer worked until his death in July, 1942, on the interpretation of this material, and many of the articles remain as he had written them. Upon his death, his work was continued by Sir Frank Stenton and Professor Bruce Dickins. Since the summer of 1946, when Sir Frank Stenton resigned from the co-editorship of the Society's volumes, that responsibility has devolved on Professor Dickins alone. In the later stages of the work the authors have had the generous help of scholars, our indebtedness to whom is expressed below.

The arrangement of the volumes under wards is based on that given in Nicolson and Burn's *The History and Antiquities of the counties of Westmorland and Cumberland*. The parishes are the civil parishes of the 6-inch Ordnance Survey sheets, since the publication of which there have been many changes in parish boundaries. It is hoped, however, that the list of parishes as key to the map printed after the Indexes will help readers towards identification. For the first time in this series, the field and unidentified names are printed at the end of each parish, instead of in a separate section at the end of the volume. These names are arranged in two groups, (*a*) those which are in current use or which are recorded after 1800, and (*b*) those which are not recorded after 1799. The latest recorded names are given first, with any earlier reference to the name given in brackets after it.

The Place-Names of Cumberland has been for so many years in preparation that we owe a debt of gratitude for help in various ways to an exceptionally large number of people both in and beyond the county. If, over the course of years, the names of some of these have inadvertently been omitted from the lists which follow, we would ask their forgiveness.

To Mr T. Gray, formerly Librarian and Curator of the Public Library, Museum and Art Gallery at Tullie House, Carlisle, our debt is incalculable. It is hardly too much to say that but for him these volumes might never have appeared. When University College, London, was partly destroyed by enemy action in September, 1940, Mr Gray very kindly took charge at Tullie House of all the material which then existed for the future *Place-Names of Cumberland*. Since work on this county began in 1931, Mr Gray has lent books, suggested new sources of material, both printed and unprinted, allowed us to consult unprinted documents at Tullie House and gained for us access to other manuscript collections in the county, read the typescript and the proofs of that part of the volumes which relates to the district round Carlisle, made many valuable corrections and additions to these, and has answered innumerable questions with unfailing courtesy and with seemingly unwearied patience.

As in other counties, we asked in Cumberland for the help of the local education authority in the work of collecting lists of modern field-names. Mr G. B. Brown, then Director of Education for the county, gave us his ready co-operation, and we would record our gratitude to him. The appeal to the schools was made at a difficult time, when the staffs were faced with war-time problems, and though only a few schools were able to help us, that help was of great value. We should like to thank the staff and pupils of the following schools for the work they did on our behalf: Samuel King's Secondary School, Alston; Bewcastle Park School; Blencogo School; Bowness-on-Solway School; Bromfield School; St Patrick's Boys' School, Cleator Moor; Keswick School; Melmerby School; Skirwith School and Wreay School.

To the following landowners and others we would express our gratitude for giving us access to documents in their possession or custody: Mr G. W. Graham-Bowman (Bishops' Registers, and documents belonging to the Duke of Devonshire, Sir Fergus Graham of Netherby and the Mounsey-Heysham family); the Bishop of Carlisle; the Dean and Chapter of Carlisle; the Earl of Carlisle; Mrs I. M. Chance (Curwen deeds at Workington); Captain Anthony Crofton; the Ecclesiastical Commissioners; Messrs Hough, Halton and Soal of Carlisle (Brisco and Holm Cultram Court Rolls); Canon Harrison (York Minster archives); Mrs T. Hartley; the Lady Henley; Mr R. H.

Hodgkin and the Fellows of The Queen's College, Oxford; the late
Camilla, Lady Lawson; Lord Leconfield; the late Earl of Lonsdale;
the Duke of Norfolk; the late Lady Cecilia Roberts; Mrs Sanderson
and Colonel G. Pocklington Senhouse.

The proofs have been read by people in the county who by their
knowledge of local documents and local topography have enabled us
to avoid many pitfalls. In this connection we owe a debt of great
gratitude to the Rev. C. M. Lowther Bouch; Mr F. R. Burnett;
Mr W. G. C. Donald; Miss M. C. Fair (who has also given us most
generous help in archaeological and other problems in the Eskdale
district); the Lady Henley (who, in addition to giving us access to
the documents at Boothby, has, from the early days of the work,
placed unstintingly at our disposal her great knowledge of the
topography, dialect and lore of the northern part of the county);
Mr C. Roy Hudleston (to whom we also owe forms from Hudleston
deeds and other manuscript sources); the Rev. Dr J. R. H. Moorman;
the late Mr R. Morton Rigg; the Rev. F. B. Swift and the late
Rev. W. S. Sykes (who supplied us with much material for South
Cumberland).

We have also to express our indebtedness to those scholars outside
the county who have read the proofs, and without whose criticisms
and suggestions the volumes would have been much the poorer. They
are Professor Eilert Ekwall, Mr J. E. B. Gover (who furnished us
with much comparative material from Cornwall), Professor Hugh
Smith, Dr Dorothy Whitelock, Professor Sir Ifor Williams and
Professor Kenneth Jackson.

Lord Lonsdale allowed us to have a new photograph made of
Gospatric's writ, and to reproduce it. The list of those who have helped
us in various other ways is a long one. Where possible, the nature of
the help given has been indicated. But to all of them our debt is great
Miss Y. Adamson (Alston minor names); the late Mr T. Barnes
(Lowther documents); Mr M. Bell (Naworth documents); the late
Mr T. Blacklock (Cockermouth documents); Mr and Mrs F. R. Burnett
(Seascale and Eskdale names, and hospitality, without which much of
the work done on manuscript collections in the county would not have
been possible); Miss Caddle (documents in the Diocesan Registry);
Miss I. Churchill (forms from Hudleston deeds); the late Professor
R. G. Collingwood (lending notes made by the late Professor W. G.
Collingwood); Mrs Crawford (field-names in Bowness on Solway);
the Rev. J. C. Dickinson (sometime Editor of the *Transactions of the*

Cumberland and Westmorland Antiquarian and Archaeological Society);
Messrs Fisher, Sanders and Co. of Market Harborough (field-names
in the Fletcher-Vane estates); the late Colonel J. F. Haswell (Penrith
names); Miss K. Hodgson (field-names in Crosby-on-Eden); Miss
F. A. Husbands (Brayton documents); the late Mr W. James (minor
names in the Naworth district); the late Mr W. T. McIntire; the late
Colonel D. J. Mason (Lowther documents at Whitehaven); Mr H. C.
Pinckney (Cockermouth documents); Miss E. S. Scroggs (checking
Tithe Award references); Miss M. Snaith (for much help in connection
with work on documents and books at Tullie House); Lady Stenton
(Pipe Roll references); the late Professor J. Tait (Eskdale names);
Mr B. L. Thompson (field-names in National Trust property); Miss
Joan Wake (lending her transcript of the Hesleyside deeds); Mr S.
Walton (Boothby documents); Mr R. C. Wilton (documents at Norfolk
House); Mr A. C. Wood (for forms from unprinted sources, and,
during the war, for checking references to documents in the Public
Record Office).

For much patience and great help we are indebted to the staffs
of the Public Record Office; the British Museum; Tullie House,
Carlisle; the Library of University College, London; the Library
of University College of Wales, Aberystwyth; the National Library
of Wales; Dr Williams' Library; the Institute of Historical Research;
the Library of the University of Reading, and the University Library,
Cambridge; and, above all, to Miss Margaret Midgley, who has been
the Society's research assistant since 1946.

The map has been drawn by Mr W. H. G. Dickins of Corpus
Christi College, Cambridge, now Lecturer in Geography at Saltley
College, Birmingham.

We are, as always in the volumes in this series, indebted to the
Cambridge University Press for the skill and care with which they
print from particularly difficult typescript.

THE EDITORS

CAMBRIDGE
24 *May* 1951–10 *April* 1952

CONTENTS

INTRODUCTION

THE GEOGRAPHY OF CUMBERLAND

Cumberland 'land of the Cymry' is bounded on the west by the Irish Sea and on the north at first by the Solway Firth as far as Sarkfoot. The boundary then runs up the Sark to the Scots Dyke, then more or less east along the Dyke to the Esk, then up the Liddel and Kershope Burn to the north-east angle of the county. The eastern boundary runs for the most part across wild fells, following a tributary of the Irthing and then the Irthing itself as far as the Haltwhistle Gap through which pass Agricola's Stane Street and Hadrian's Wall. Then come wild fells again to the south-east angle of the county and of Alston parish which lies east of the divide. Thence the southern boundary runs up the headwaters of the Tees, then roughly south-west to the Eden, down the Eden to the Eamont, up the Eamont to Ullswater, along Ullswater almost to the head, then very roughly south-west to the Duddon and down the Duddon to the sea.

The county does not represent an old kingdom like Kent, Sussex or Essex in the South-East, nor the district dependent on a Danish *here* like several of the East Midland counties. Nor is it a self-contained geographical region, being merely the north-western half of the region which comprises Cumberland, Westmorland and Lancashire North-of-the-Sands and is styled Cumbria by modern geographers[1]. It falls into three main areas:

(1) The north-western half of the Cumbrian Dome, with its narrow coastal strip. Here the percentage of arable varies from 2, in the central fell parishes, to at least 75, on the New Red Sandstone of the coastal strip from Drigg Point to a little north of St Bees Head. Thence to the far side of the Eden valley lie the Coal Measures. The iron ore on which the industrial development of West Cumberland is based is found in two main areas, one lying south of the middle Ehen round Cleator (357) and Egremont (379), the other in the south-west tip of the county (the Millom (414) district).

(2) The Eden Lowland (down which has run the main road from the south, at any rate since Roman times), together with the sheep pastures on the Carboniferous Limestone of the Pennine Slopes.

---

[1] See *Great Britain: Essays in Regional Geography*, ed. A. O. Ogilvie, pp. 349–67, Cambridge 1930.

(3) The Carlisle Plain (watered by the lower Eden and its tributaries and by the Wampool and the Waver), together with the pastoral slopes, also of Carboniferous Limestone, entered from the east by the Haltwhistle Gap. In the lowland areas the percentage of arable is from 30 to over 50, and farming is of the mixed type—oats, turnips, swedes, and sown grasses, with much milk production and raising and fattening of cattle.

THE WARDS OF CUMBERLAND

In Southern and Western England the unit between the parish and the shire was the hundred, in the Scandinavian settlements usually the wapentake, while Yorkshire and the Parts of Lindsey had an intermediate division into three ridings (þriðiungar). The four Northern counties were however divided into wards[1] (balli(v)æ in Latin), as were certain shires in the South of Scotland[2], where Lanarkshire still finds a use for its Upper, Middle and Lower Wards as minor administrative units. Cumberland was divided into Eskdale, Cumberland, Leath, Allerdale below Derwent and Allerdale above Derwent Wards; Westmorland into East, West, Kendal and Kirkby Lonsdale Wards; Northumberland into Glendale[3], Bamburgh, Coquetdale, Morpeth, Castle and Tindale Wards, plus the Liberties of Norham and Islandshire, Bedlingtonshire, Bellingham and Redesdale (which last is sometimes styled a Ward); County Durham into Chester (le-Street), Darlington, Easington and Stockton Wards. It is from County Durham that the earliest reference to these ballivæ is observed in the Close Rolls for 1237. The Cumberland Wards are apparently first recorded under Edward I (Cumberland Assize Rolls 6 Edw. I, No. 132, m. 32 d and 20 Edw. I, No. 135, m. 17 d).

Again as in Southern Scotland, where Ettrick Forest was divided into Tweed, Yarrow and Ettrick Wards, the Forest of Inglewood[4]

---

[1] G. Neilson, *Juridical Review* xi, 82 n.

[2] *Ward* is derived from OE *w(e)ard*, and here the original sense is presumably 'district to which certain defensive duties are assigned.'

[3] Still smaller wards are to be observed in the parish of Elsdon, which has a sixfold division into Elsdon, Monkridge, Otterburn, (High) Rochester, Troughend and Woodside Wards.

[4] Hesket in the Forest (199) and Hutton-in-the-Forest (208), both in Inglewood Forest, are so called to distinguish them from Hesket Newmarket (277) and Hutton John, Roof and Soil (210–14) respectively.

had its wards, and it is from one of these that Westward parish (329) takes its name. In Derbyshire too there were Belper, Campana and Colebrook Wards in the Peak Forest[1].

To complete the story, a paragraph on the ward as a division of city or borough may not be out of place. All the earliest quotations in NED refer to the City of London wards, for which there is no direct evidence before the reign of Henry I. But such divisions existed in some English boroughs before the Conquest. In Edward the Confessor's day there were *custodiæ*[2] in Cambridge (ten, of which one had, by the compilation of Domesday Book, been wiped out in the building of the Castle) and Stamford (six). Presumably similar were the *scyræ*[3] of York (seven, of which one had by 1086 been wiped out in the building of the Castle) and *ferlingi*[4] of Huntingdon. It is this use of ward that is most familiar to-day in Great Britain and in the U.S.A., where *ward-politician* has no sweet savour.

THE ROMAN AND BRITISH PERIODS

Nothing is known of the area from written sources before Agricola (77–83), though it is probable enough that it formed part of the territory of the Celtic people called Brigantes. Under their queen Cartismandua the Brigantes had played the Roman game during the Caratacus campaigns that ended in 51. Their turn came twenty years later when the Emperor Vespasian appointed as governor of Britain Q. Petillius Cerialis, who in three years (71–4) completed the reduction of the eastern uplands of Yorkshire; he, or his successor Frontinus, established the fortress of York, to which the Legion IX Hispana was moved up from Lincoln. Sex. Iulius Frontinus turned his attention to Wales, and it was not till Cn. Iulius Agricola took over that the northward advance was resumed. In 78, 79 and 80 Agricola carried the Roman frontier to Forth and Clyde, and established a chain of forts across the isthmus. Operations in the Irish Sea, for which it is possible that he built the naval base at *Clanoventa* (Ravenglass, 425), took up 81, and Agricola's northern expeditions

---

[1] See generally NED, which does not however recognise the English use of *ward* as a division of a forest, and O. S. Anderson, *The English Hundred Names* (Lund 1934), pp. xxiv–xxvi, which adduces no Scots material.

[2] In Leviticus viii, 35, *custodias* is rendered *wearde* (acc.sg.fem.).

[3] OE *scīr*, 'division,' now specialised in the sense of 'county.'

[4] OE *fēorþling*, 'quarter.'

of the next two years, for all their spectacular success, produced no lasting result[1].

Of the two most striking monuments of Roman rule in Cumberland the *Stanegate*, or *Carelgate* 'road to Carlisle,' was constructed by Agricola's troops. In 122-6 Hadrian's Wall[2] was built under A. Platorius Nepos after a serious rising of the native peoples. In the last decade of that century D. Clodius Albinus denuded the province of troops for his campaign against Severus, and the barbarians carried their devastations as far south as York and Chester. Once Severus had gained the upper hand he re-established Hadrian's Wall, and for about a century there was peace till Allectus (293-6) stripped it once again of its garrison. His successful rival Constantius Chlorus, who died in 305, had in great measure to rebuild the Wall. Again came a period of peace till 367, when the Picts, joined by the Scots from Ireland, inflicted a fearful defeat on the Roman forces and the Wall had to be reconstructed a third time by Count Theodosius, who, however, abandoned the outlying forts such as BANNA (Bewcastle 60). Military occupation can be traced till 383, when for the last time troops were withdrawn by Magnus Maximus.

As elsewhere in the Highland Zone the Roman occupation was of a military character, and there is little evidence of its effect on the native population, which is unlikely to have been very numerous. Practically all the sites so far excavated are on the Wall or on the coastline, or are fortified posting stations on military roads. On the other hand LVGVVALIVM (Carlisle) does not appear to have been military in character. A defensible site in a fertile valley, it has, from the earliest times, been marked out for human settlement, since the Petteril and the Caldew join the Eden within a mile of each other, and the peninsula formed by the three rivers rises gently from the south till it falls abruptly towards the Eden[3]. As a Roman site it was certainly occupied in Flavian times, probably under Agricola. The site of PETRIANAE is at Stanwix across the river from Carlisle.

Of the handful of Romano-British place-names recorded in classical

[1] For the chronology of Agricola's campaigns see J. G. C. Anderson's edition of Tacitus' *Agricola*, pp. 166-73 (Oxford 1922), and I. A. Richmond, *Journal of Roman Studies* xxxiv, 34-45.

[2] The tenth edition, revised by I. A. Richmond (Newcastle-upon-Tyne 1947), of J. Collingwood Bruce's *Handbook to the Roman Wall* marks a great advance. For the general history of Roman Britain see R. G. Collingwood and J. N. L. Myres, *Roman Britain and the English Settlements* (Oxford 1936).

[3] For a town-site analysis of Carlisle see Alice Garnett, *The Geographical Interpretation of Topographical Maps* (London 1930), pp. 152-8.

or post-classical sources, one only[1], LVGVVALIVM (Carlisle), is repre-
sented on the modern map, but Walby (76) and Walton (114),
Wallhead and Wallfoot (111) derive their first element from Hadrian's
Wall, from which Oldwall (93) is also named. Old Penrith in
Plumpton Wall (235) is the site of VOREDA. The stone walls of
PETRIANAE give its name to Stanwix (108). The *burh* in Burgh by
Sands (126) is the fort of ABALLAVA, and the *caer* in Cardurnock (123)
is a Roman coastal fortlet in the construction of which cobble-stones
were much in evidence. The *Castle* of Castlesteads (114) refers to
the Roman fort of VXELLODVNVM on the Wall. It should be added
that ALAVNA and DERVENTIO, which are now identified with the
Roman sites at Ellenborough (284) and Papcastle (308), are really
river-names represented to-day by the Ellen and the Derwent[2].

THE BRITISH REVIVAL

Since Constantine the garrison had been, nominally at all events,
Christian, though no evidence of Christian worship has so far come
to light on the Wall. Whether the native population was even
nominally Christian at the end of the fourth century is more than
one can say. After the final evacuation of the Wall they came under
the rule of British princes, and there is some evidence that Cumberland
formed part of the kingdom of Rheged. Urien of Rheged, who,
according to the "Saxon Genealogies" appended to Nennius, was,
with Rhydderch ap Tudwal of Strathclyde[3], one of the four British
princes who opposed the Bernician king Hussa, and himself beset
Hussa's brother Theodric for three days and nights in Holy Island,
apparently ruled in Carlisle. Urien was the subject of several of the
Taliesin poems[4], in which he is styled 'prince of *Catraeth*' (Catterick),
and that suggests that his kingdom extended a good deal further to
the south-east. There is, however, only one historical fact that relates
to sixth-century Cumberland and can be precisely dated—the defeat

[1] The name Moricambe (291), like Morecambe Bay (PN La 176) is due to an
antiquarian itch to identify the bay mentioned by Ptolemy. For the Romano-
British place-names that certainly, or probably, fall within the county see Appendix
(pp. 509–12).
[2] For the identifications (some still hotly disputed) of Romano-British names in
Cumberland see Appendix (pp. 510–11).
[3] Rhydderch *Hen* 'the Old,' later styled *Hael* 'the Bountiful,' is mentioned by
Adamnan (*Vita S. Columbae* I, 15) as a friend of St Columba and as living at
Petra Cloithe, now Dumbarton 'fortress of the Britons.'
[4] See J. Morris Jones, "Taliesin" (*Y Cymmrodor* xxviii), especially pp. 64–71
Urien's son Owain is also the subject of one of the Taliesin poems.

at *Arfderydd* in 573 of Gwenddoleu ap Ceidio, whose name is perhaps
preserved in Carwinley (52) near Arthuret, with which *Arfderydd*
can safely be identified. What they fought each other for has been the
subject of much speculation[1], to which I do not propose to add.
It is enough to say that the area may, at that time, have been in need
of evangelisation or re-evangelisation, for the work of St Kentigern,
to whom are dedicated the Cumberland churches of Irthington,
Grinsdale, Bromfield, Aspatria, Caldbeck, Castle Sowerby, Mungrisdale and Crosthwaite[2], is ascribed to the period after *Arfderydd*.
As late as 1258, well after the establishment of a see at Carlisle, the
bishop of Glasgow, who claimed to be St Kentigern's successor,
pretended to authority over all the old lands of the Cymry as far to
the south-east as the Rere Cross on Stainmoor in Westmorland[3].

Wherever the historical Arthur may have lived and carried on his
struggle against the Saxon invader, the legendary Arthur is not
associated with Cumberland in Geoffrey of Monmouth, nor in Wace
and Laȝamon. Later however there is a group of Middle English
romances belonging to the Arthurian cycle and having their scene
laid in Carlisle[4], or the Forest of Inglewood (where very odd things
might happen), or both. The association of Arthur's court with Carlisle
is at least as old as Marie de France, who wrote in the reign of
Henry II, and Chrestien de Troyes, whose *Yvain*[5] has been dated
between 1170 and 1175, and it has been argued, as by Heinrich
Zimmer[6], that it reflects a tradition of the days when the Cymry

[1] See W. F. Skene, *Celtic Scotland* i, 156–9 (Edinburgh 1876). On the genealogies
of the *Gwŷr y Gogledd* 'Men of the North' see Skene, *The Four Ancient Books of
Wales* i, 165–85 (Edinburgh 1868), and J. E. Lloyd, *A History of Wales from the
earliest times to the Edwardian Conquest* i, 165–7 (London 1939). According to the
Annales Cambriæ, s.a. 573, Gwenddoleu's opponents were the sons of Elifer,
Gwenddoleu's uncle in the Genealogies.
Other place-names preserving British personal names that may date from this
period are Carnetley (84) and *Couwhencatte* (71), the site of which was apparently
in Burtholme; these may contain *Teiliau* and *Guencat*.
[2] The parish church of Keswick, perhaps the *Crosfeld, id est Crucis Novale*,
of Jocelyn of Furness' life of the Saint, c. xxiii. On the dedication of Cumberland
churches generally see CW xxv, 1–37. For a list of springs, etc., bearing saints'
names, *v.* Index *infra*.
[3] *Chronicon de Lanercost*, ed. J. Stevenson, p. 65.
[4] In the Alliterative *Morte Arthure* (vv. 64 ff.) the king holds his Christmas court
in Carlisle.
[5] *Le Lai de Lanval*, vv. 5–8; *Yvain*, v. 7. On the former is based the ME *Landeval*,
on the latter the northern ME *Ywain and Gawain*, in which however *Carduel an
Gales* becomes *Kerdyf, þat es in Wales* (v. 17).
[6] *Göttingische gelehrte Anzeigen* (1890), pp. 525–7.

ruled in Cumberland. In almost all of the romances for which a Cumberland setting is provided, Sir Gawain plays an important part. *The Awntyrs off Arthure at the Terne Wathelyne* (probably written in the North of England between 1350 and 1400) knows Carlisle, the Forest of Inglewood (38), Tarn Wadling (204) and the Court Thorn (202) hard by. Of similar date, and also from the Ireland Manuscript formerly at Hale Hall near Liverpool[1], is *The Avowynge of King Arthur*, which is laid in the same area. *The Weddynge of Sir Gawen*, rather later and from further south, begins with a hunt in the Forest; on this is based *The Marriage of Sir Gawaine* in Bishop Percy's Folio Manuscript. *Syre Gawene and the Carle of Carelyle*, a tail-rime romance of the fourteenth or fifteenth century, has similarly been turned into a ballad of the sixteenth, *The Carle off Carlile*, also in the Folio Manuscript. In the same MS is *Sir Lambewell*, which is based on the ME *Sir Landeval*; in *Sir Lambewell* King Arthur holds his court in "merry Carlile"[2].

Most of the more, and many of the less, important river- and stream-names are Celtic or pre-Celtic in origin—Cairn Beck, Calder, Cam Beck, Cammock Beck (148), Chalk Beck, Cocker, Crummock Beck, Dacre Beck, Derwent, Eden, Ellen, the two Esks, Glencoyne Beck, Hether Burn, Irt, Irthing, Knorren Beck, Lyne, Mite, Nent, South Tyne with its humbler namesake *Tyne Sike* (a name once applied to Dog Beck). But it should not be forgotten that, apart from some minor streams, Caldew, Duddon, Eamont, Liddel Water and Waver were named by Anglian settlers; Aira Beck, Bleng, Croglin, Greta, Ive, Keekle, Liza, Roe Beck and Skill Beck, to which should be added the first element of Lorton (408), by men of Scandinavian speech. For the rest, Dacre (186) is an old river-name, and of hill-names Barrock (201) and Mell (212), with its diminutive preserved in Watermillock (254), are British. Hill-names are not often recorded in early sources, but British elements signifying 'rock,' as *carn*[3], *carrecc*[4] and *creic*[5], or some other prominent topographical feature,

---

[1] Now in the Bodmer Library, Cologny, Switzerland.

[2] The romances provide a few medieval forms for names that are otherwise poorly recorded. For further details see J. E. Wells, *A Manual of the Writings in Middle English 1050–1400*. The romances of which Sir Gawain is the hero were conveniently assembled by Sir Frederic Madden in 1839.

Why should Carlisle, like Wakefield in the West Riding, be styled 'merry'?

[3] 'heap of stones,' in Cairn Beck (6), Carnetley (84), Blencarn (214).

[4] 'rock,' in Carrock Fell (305), Cargo (94), *Karcmurdath* (91).

[5] 'rock,' in Greystoke (195), Crakeplace (367), Blindcrake (266).

as those corresponding to Modern Welsh *blaen*[1], *cadair*[2], *coed*[3], *crug*[4], *culdir*[5], *cwm*[6], *dôl*[7], *drum*[8], *glyn*[9], *llanerch*[10], *maen*[11], *mynydd*[12], *pen*[13], *perth*[14], *rhos*[15], *rhyd*[16], *tal*[17], *tir*[18], *tor*[19], are prominent in compounds of pre-English origin. Other terms of British origin are those corresponding to Modern Welsh *buarth*[20], *burdd*[21], *caer*[22], *cil*[23], *tref*[24]. If river-names be left out of consideration the pre-English element is particularly in evidence in three areas:

(1) In Eskdale Ward, mainly on the rising ground to the north and east of Carlisle.

(2) In Leath Ward, in the foothills that lie between the Vale of Eden and the Skiddaw massif.

(3) In Allerdale below Derwent Ward, some way inland, on the high ground between the rivers Ellen and Derwent.

It is surprisingly scanty in the Dome itself—less noticeable in fact than in the coastal lowlands, where we find Holm Cultram (288), Newton Arlosh (291) and Coulderton (413).

---

[1] 'top,' in Blencogo (122), Blencow (186), Blencarn (214), Blencathra (253), Blennerhasset (265).

[2] 'chair,' in Catterlen (182), *Caterlaising* (271).

[3] 'wood,' in Clesketts (84), Culgaith (184).

[4] 'hill,' in Gilcrux (287), Cumcrook (59).

[5] 'narrow strip of land,' in Coulderton (413), Holm Cultram (288).

[6] 'valley,' in Cumcrook (59), Cumcatch (66), *Couwhencatte* (71), Cumrew (77), Cumwhitton (78), Cumrenton (92), Cumdivock (132), Cumwhinton (161).

[7] 'riverside meadow,' in *Dollerline* (55).

[8] 'ridge,' in Dundraw (139), Drumburgh (124).

[9] 'valley,' in Glencoyne (15), Glen Dhu (61).

[10] 'glade,' in Lanercost (71), *Lanrekaythin* (72), and probably Lanerton (115).

[11] 'stone,' in Triermain (116), Redmain (267), and probably Temon (81).

[12] 'mountain,' in Tarnmonath (87).

[13] 'head,' in *Pendraven* (82), Penruddock (213), Penrith (229), Torpenhow (325).

[14] 'bush,' in Parton (156), Solport (107).

[15] 'high ground,' in *Raswraget* (103).

[16] 'ford,' in Redmain (267), Penrith (229).

[17] 'brow,' in Talkin (88), Tallentire (324).

[18] 'land,' in Tallentire (324) and *culdir* above.

[19] 'peak,' in Tercrosset (97), Torpenhow (325).

[20] 'fold,' in Burtholme (70).

[21] 'table,' in Birdoswald (115).

[22] 'fortress,' in Carwinley (52), Cardunneth (77), Cardurnock (123), Cardew (131), *Caraverick* (202), and probably in Caermote (326). An adjectival form appears in Castle Carrock (74).

[23] 'retreat,' in Culgaith (184), Gilcrux (287).

[24] 'homestead,' in Triermain (116).

The Anglian Period

There are two obvious lines of penetration from the south—down the Vale of Eden to Carlisle, and along the coastal strip that fringes the mountains of the Dome. No example of *-ing*, nor of *-ingas*, has been noted in Cumberland, and the proportion of Anglian names of demonstrably early type is very small. Earliest are Addingham (193), on the upper Eden, Whicham (443) and Hensingham (400), in the coastal strip. Pretty certainly antedating the Scandinavian invasion are Brigham (355), Dearham (283), and (Holm) Cultram (288)[1], and the *ing(a)tūn* names Rottington (428), Frizington (336), Distington (375), Harrington (399) and Workington (454), all in the coastal strip, or on rivers at no great distance from the sea. Other names that may be reasonably early are Muncaster (423), Irton (402) on the Irt, Gosforth (393), Coulderton (413), Arlecdon (335), Cockermouth (361) on the Cocker, Camerton (281), Ellenborough (284) and Hayton (288), all in the coastal strip and mostly at no great height. To these may be added Waverton (159) on the Waver, Wigton (166), Sebergham (150), Dalston (130), Bowness (123), Burgh by Sands (126) and Warwick (157) in or adjoining the Carlisle Plain, Kirklinton (101) and Bewcastle (60) up the Lyne valley, and Hayton (88), Irthington (91), Brampton (65), Farlam (83), Walton (114) and the Dentons (81) in the basin of the Irthing[2]. Good farmland was what attracted the Anglian settler, and there is no evidence that the British occupation of the Lakeland hills was seriously challenged till the Norwegians came from Ireland. An area between the middle Eden and the divide may similarly have remained a British fastness. The parishes of Castle Carrock (74) and Cumrew (77) still bear names of British origin, and the forms of Carlatton (73) and Cumwhitton (78), the adjoining parishes, strongly suggest that territories once occupied by the Anglian invader may have been recovered, after an interval, by their earlier owners.

It is likely that by the end of the first quarter of the seventh century the Northumbrians had made a good deal of progress in Cumbria. Bede (*Historia Ecclesiastica* i, 34) says that Æthelfrith conquered more territories from the Britons than any other chieftain or king,

---

[1] Incidentally Brigham (302) and Hestham (415) had, in the first instance, *-holmr* as their second element.

[2] Irton, Cockermouth, Ellenborough, Linton and Irthington have all as first element a British river-name. For Coulderton v. *supra* 413.

either subduing the inhabitants and making them tributary, or driving them out and planting the English in their places. Alarmed at this, Aedan macGabrain, "king of the Scots that dwell in Britain" (that is of the Scots of Dalriada, whose lands did not march with those of the Northumbrians), attacked Æthelfrith in 603 and suffered a crushing defeat. Now, or at any rate in the course of the seventh century, Northumbrian power extended to the Solway and beyond. Carlisle, which may have been continuously occupied by the Cymry since Roman days, was firmly in Northumbrian hands by 685. A nunnery, at the head of which was a member of the royal house, had been established, and ecclesiastically the area was dependent on Lindisfarne, to which Carlisle and a circuit of fifteen miles round (perhaps represented by the old parish of St Cuthbert Without (147)) was granted by Ecgfrith. The defeat and death of Ecgfrith on his northern adventure of 685 put a period to Northumbrian expansion. If the very questionable reading of the Bewcastle inscription be accepted, the Cross presumably dates from before the disaster. The closely related Ruthwell Cross, which can on linguistic grounds be assigned to the early eighth century, is a massive and striking monument which hardly suggests a tottering society. Apart from Bewcastle there are in Cumberland remains of Anglian sculpture not later than the ninth century, at Carlisle (two, one of which is inscribed), Workington (two), Irton (a fine cross), Waberthwaite (near Muncaster) and Addingham (two); these are all in places at which we could, on other grounds, have postulated early Anglian settlement[1]. Carlisle therefore, and the less mountainous parts of Cumbria, remained in Northumbrian hands for more than two centuries after the disaster of Dunnichen. The Danish Halfdan's raids on Strathclyde (ASC 875) may have shaken Northumbrian authority in the North-West, but there is no convincing evidence that his people's settlements east of the Pennines had dealt it a death-blow.

THE IRISH-SCANDINAVIAN SETTLEMENT

The threat to North-West England came rather from the west, from Ireland or the Isle of Man. Very early in the tenth century there was a Scandinavian settlement on the Wirral peninsula of Cheshire. Further north there was still at that time a *princeps* (*ealdorman* or *hēahgerēfa*, call him what you will, in the vernacular)

---

[1] Cf. W. S. Calverley, *Notes on the Early Sculptured Crosses of the old diocese of Carlisle* (Kendal 1899), alphabetically arranged.

who had to flee eastwards over the moors some time, probably not long, before 915. This was perhaps the time, rather than 875, when Carlisle was laid in ruins, after which, it is alleged, it remained deserted for two hundred years—if indeed Florence of Worcester had anything more than the *Anglo-Saxon Chronicle* for 875 and 1092 to guide him.

The settlers in Cumbria were Norwegians by descent but much modified in speech by their stay in a Gaelic-speaking area. Instead of forming their place-names in the normal Scandinavian (and English) way they inverted the order of compounds, placing the defined term first after the Irish fashion illustrated by Downpatrick and Ballymurphy[1]. The following is, it is hoped, a reasonably complete list of names[2] (arranged under their first element) which can be regarded as falling within the category:

askr	Aspatria 261.
bekkr	*Becblenekar* (Blencarn Beck or Crowdundale Beck) 5. *Becblencarn* (Crowdundale Beck), Beckermet 337, *Beckfarlam* (Farlam Beck) 14, Beckfellican 247, *Becksenowyate* 395, *Beksneuell* 390, *Becksonen* 421, *Becstervild* 218, *Becsnari* (Snary Beck) 27, *bek Troyte* (Wiza Beck) 31, *Bechwythop* (Wythop Beck) 31.
? brenke	Burntippet 84.
brycg or *bryggja*	Bridge Petton 394, *Briggethorfin* 360.
bú	Bewaldeth 264.
búðir	Brotherilkeld 343.
castel	Castelyadolfbek 253.
croft	*Croftbathoc* 444, *Croftbladen* 420, Croftmorris 421.
dalr	Dalemain 186, *Dale Raghon beck* (Hazelrigg Beck) 17.
eign	Aynthorfin 360.
eik	Aykcrist 185.
fit	Fitbrandan 360.
gil	Gillcambon 196, *Gillefinchor* 412, Gilgarran 375.
haugr	Hou Groucok 396, How Michael 456.
*hobb(e)	Hobcarton 408.
hofuð	*Hovedgleuermerhe* 350, *Hovedscaldale* 351.
holmr	*Holweri* 43, *holme Camok* 171.

[1] The problem of inversion compounds is treated in detail by E. Ekwall, *Scandinavians and Celts in the North-West of England* (Lund 1918).

[2] A glance at the accompanying map will show better than a lengthy description the distribution of the type.

kirkia	Kirkandrews 99, 141, 185, Kirkbride 144, *Kirkbrynnok* 62, Kirkoswald 215, Kirksanton 415.
kirkiubýr	*Kirkebibeccoch* 430, *Kirkeby Crossan* 436.
kelda	Keldhouse 169.
krossi	*Croscrin* 218, ? Crosslacon 337.
moldi	Mockerkin 410.
sætr	*Satgodard* 344, Seatallan 442, Seatoller 351, *Seteknoc* 397, *Setforn'* 426, Setmabanning 313, Setmurthy 433.
skálir	Scarrowmanwick 250, *Skalmallok* 269.
snab	*Snabmurris* 367.
steinn	Stanbrennan 339, *Staynlenoc* 417.
stīg or *stígr*	Stibenet 253, *Styalein* 411.
þveit	*Thueitdounegaleg'* 403.
tiǫrn	*Tarngunerigg* 456, Tarn Wadling 204, *Ternmeran* (Mockerkin Tarn) 34.
varði	*Warthcreggele* 117, *Watchcomon* 103.

Apart from *Castelyadolfbek* the examples cited above have, certainly or probably, a Germanic first element. The second element is Germanic in Knock Murton (406), *Lakewolf* (134), *Karkebucholm* (450), and there is possibly a Norman personal name in Knockupworth (141). That the practice long survived is shown by the names Hall Bolton and Hallsenna (394), Hall Santon (402), Hallthwaites (417) and Hall Waberthwaite (439). Anywhere but in the North-West these would be Waberthwaite Hall, etc.

A second type of name that shows Irish-Scandinavian influence in Cumberland is the *-erg* compound, containing a loanword from Irish *airigh*, 'shieling.' These are chiefly to be found in Allerdale above Derwent, as Birker (342), Cleator (357), *Crokerbec* (10, 450), Langley (365), Mosser (422), *Helewynherge* (397), *Ravenerhals*, now Buttermere Hause (355), Salter (432), Stephney (339), Winder (406 and probably 399), and, probably, Glaramara (350). There are however three examples in Leath Ward, Berrier (181), Hewer Hill (245), and Stockdalewath (246). The type is not found at all in the north and east of the county, even in the eastern fringe where the elevations are considerable and the terrain is appropriate.

Goidelic personal names, doubtless for the most part introduced from Ireland, are commonest in Allerdale above Derwent. Those that seem reasonably well authenticated are Brandán in *Fitbrandan* (360), Cartán in Hobcarton (408), Cros(s)án in *Kirkeby Crossan* (436),

Corc in *Korkgill* (426), Corcán in Mockerkin (410), Dungal in *Thueitdounegaleg'* (403), Gearrán in Gilgarran (375), Gillamuire in *Gilmoreboug* (436), Gille in *Gillecroft* (446), Gillamicháil in *Gillemihelecroft* (446), Glas in Ravenglass (425), Lennóc in *Staynlenoc* (417), Lochán in Laconby (396), Murdoch (Muiredach) in Setmurthy (433), Suthán in Greysouthen (397). Leath has again a few—Cambán in Gillcambon (196), Crín in *Croscrin* (218), Glas(s)án in Glassonby (194), Melmor (Maelmuire) in Melmerby (223), and possibly Mungo in Mungrisdale (226). There are fewer still in Allerdale below Derwent—Dubhán in Dovenby (284), Mabannán in Setmabanning (313), Patric in Aspatria (261) and possibly Macóg in *Skalmallok* (269). The Gaels who have left their names in Eskdale and Cumberland Wards are just as likely to have come from the North at a later period, as seems to have been the case with Bueth and his son Gille after whom Boothby (65) and Gilsland (2) are called. Other examples are Corc in Corby (161), Gilleceartáin in *Gillkertinges wathe* (129), Gillamáirtin in *Gilmartyn Riddyng* (157), Linán in Drumleaning (119), Mungo in *Mungowcroft* (137), and Murdoch in *Karcmurdath* (91).

For the rest, *búð, gil, skáli, sætr* and *þveit* are typically Norwegian[1] and the *-dales* are more likely to go back to ON *dalr* than to the cognate OE *dæl*. There are several forms which still show traces of the ON genitive singular in *-ar*, as Allerdale (1), Ennerdale (385) and Miterdale (389), 'valleys of the Ellen, Ehen and Mite' respectively[2], to which should be added Borrowdale (349) 'valley of the *borg*', Burthwaite (349), Bowderdale (440), Harter Fell (437), Stangrah (449), Waberthwaite (439), and possibly Satherton (444). The inversion compounds Brotherilkeld (343) and Scarrowmanwick (250) preserve the *-ir* of the plural *skálir*, and it is just conceivable that the *-ir* of *staðir* is still to be found in Honister (356). It will be noticed that these names, with the exception of Scarrowmanwick, are in the Ward of Allerdale above Derwent.

Further evidence for Scandinavian settlement is provided by the Gosforth Cross, with its mixture of heathen Scandinavian and Christian motives, and the stone, also from Gosforth (393), on which is carved the god Thor fishing for the world-serpent[3]. They show

---

[1] The specifically Danish *þorp* is only found in Cumberland in Cracrop (112), which is not recorded till the late sixteenth century; it appears occasionally however in Westmorland. The examples of Danish *bōð* are probably due to influence from elsewhere (ScandCelts 9).

[2] Along with these should be considered Dunnerdale 'valley of the Duddon' just across the border (PN La 223).   [3] Cf. W. S. Calverley, *op. cit.* 138ff.

that the Scandinavian mythology was known in Cumberland as in
the Isle of Man. Both are uninscribed, but the extremely odd,
though apparently genuine, 'tolfihn' *graffito* in Carlisle Cathedral
(late eleventh or early twelfth century)[1] and Richard the Mason's
legend on the Bridekirk Font (c. 1150)[2] employ the later Scandinavian
fuþork, eked out at Bridekirk (272) with five characters from the
English book-hand[3].

Whatever loose form of political organisation the Scandinavian
settlers may have had—conceivably something resembling the Ice-
landic district *thing*—the fact that Æthelstan met Constantine, King
of the Scots, and Eugenius, King of Strathclyde, *æt Eamotum* (on the
River Eamont, perhaps at Dacre) suggests that the place lay on what
was then the frontier between the English and the Strathclyde Welsh,
and that the king of the latter claimed suzerainty over Cumbria.
In 937 Eugenius was one of the Celtic-Scandinavian confederacy
defeated at *Brunanburh*, wherever that may have been; he may have
been one of the five kings slain there, as he is not heard of again.
It was in the reign of his successor Dunmail[4] that in 945 Edmund
ravaged all *Cumbraland* (presumably Strathclyde in its widest sense)[5]
and handed it over to the Scots king Malcolm I, stipulating that the
latter should co-operate with him both by land and sea. But a few
years later Dunmail was ruling in Strathclyde, and the dynasty there
only came to an end with the death of the last of his line in 1015.
Ælfric the homilist, who wrote c. 996, relates that "all the kings of
this island, of Cumbrians and Scots (*Cumbra* and *Scotta*), once came
to Edgar on a single day, and they all submitted to his direction
(*gebugon to Eadgares wissunge*)"[6]; this is practically contemporary
evidence that goes some way to corroborate Florence of Worcester,
according to whom Malcolm, King of the Cumbrians, was one of
the water party on the Dee in 973. Unhappily Edgar died in 975,
and *Cumerland* certainly did not acknowledge English authority in

[1] VCH i, 278–9.
[2] Cf. W. S. Calverley *op. cit.* 68 ff.; *Burlington Magazine* xxv, 24–9.
[3] The records of the six Viking burials so far reported from Cumberland (Hesket
in the Forest, Beacon Hill in Aspatria, Brigham, two at Eaglesfield, and West
Seaton) are discussed by J. D. Cowen, CW xlviii, 73–5, and *Archaeologia Aeliana*,
4th Series, xxvi, 55–61. All except the first-named place are in Allerdale-above-
Derwent.
[4] Dunmail Raise (312) is not recorded before 1576, but it is generally taken to be
the cairn of this Dunmail.
[5] The Annales Cambriæ, s.a. 946, record that Strathclyde (*Strat Clut*) was ravaged
by the Saxons.
[6] In the sermon on St Swithhun (*Ælfric's Lives of Saints*, ed. W. W. Skeat, i, 468).

THE GOSPATRIC WRIT

1000 when Æthelred invaded and ravaged very nearly all of it. A large part of the present county must however have been under English control for a time in the middle of the eleventh century, for Siward of Northumbria, who died in 1055 after having held the earldom for a minimum of twelve, and a maximum of fourteen, years, is associated with Gospatric of Allerdale and Dalston[1] in the earliest document that deals with Cumberland. The wording of this writ, extant only in a much mangled form in a thirteenth-century transcript that is at least a copy of a copy, suggests that in Edward the Confessor's day the district roughly defined by the Derwent (or even the South Esk), the Eamont, the central hills of northern England and the marshes at the head of the Solway was covered by the phrase "the lands that were Cumbrian"[2].

GOSPATRIC'S WRIT

Gospatric's writ is preserved among the Earl of Lonsdale's muniments at Lowther Castle, Westmorland. It was apparently known to some sixteenth- or seventeenth-century antiquarian, for, according to NB ii, 317, William Nicolson, Bishop of Carlisle, found, in a manuscript of Denton lent to him in 1708 by Mr Bird of Broughton, a Cardew pedigree headed by Thore and Thorpin (recte Thorfin) de Cardew[3]. It was not seriously discussed however till the early years of this century when it was dealt with by a number of scholars— by W. Greenwell in J. C. Hodgson's *A History of Northumberland* vii, 24–6 (Newcastle-upon-Tyne 1904), by F. W. Ragg in *The Ancestor* vii, 244–7, by James Wilson in *The Scottish Historical Review* i, 62–9, and VCH Cu ii, 231–4, by F. Liebermann (with facsimile and full linguistic notes by A. Brandl) in (*Herrigs*) *Archiv für das Studium der neueren Sprachen* cxi, 275–8, and by H. W. C. Davis in EHR xx, 61–5. It is edited, with translation and detailed commentary, by Miss Florence E. Harmer in her collection of *Anglo-Saxon Writs*, which was published by the Manchester University Press in 1952. The interested reader is referred to her treatment of the writ which I have had the privilege of seeing in page-proof. This important document is given overleaf.

[1] Probably Gospatric, son of Uhtred, the Earl of Northumbria who was murdered in 1016 (EHR xx, 61–5).

[2] It is perhaps best to take the -s of *Cōmbres* as an unusually early example of the Northern dialectal change of -sc to -s.

[3] Thore and Thorfin do not appear in any of the copies of *An Accompt of the most considerable estates and families in the County of Cumberland* by John Denton of Cardew, edited by R. S. Ferguson (Kendal 1887).

GOSPATRIC'S WRIT

Gospatrik ʒreot ealle mine ρassenas 7 hρylkun (MS hyylkun)
Mann freo 7 ðrenʒe þeo ρoonnan on eallun þam landann / þeo
ρeoron Cōmbres 7 eallun mine kynlinʒ freondlyce (MS freondlycc),
7 ic cyðe eoρ (MS eoy) þ myne mynna (MS mynua) is 7 full leof
þ Thorfynn / Mac Thore beo sρa freo on eallan ðynʒes þeo beo myne
on Alnerdall sρa ænyʒmann beo, oðer ic, oðer ænyʒ myne ρassenas,
on ρeald, on freyð, on heyninʒa, 7 æt ællun ðynʒan þeo byn eorðe
boouan (MS bœnand) 7 ðeoronder (MS -onðer) to Shauk, / to ρafyr,
to ρoll ρaðœn, to bek Troyte 7 þeo ρeald æt caldebek. 7 ic ρille þ
þeo mann bydann mið Thorfynn æt / Carðeú 7 Combedeyfoch
(MS Combeðeyfoch) beo sρa freals myð hem sρa Melmor 7 Thore
7 Syʒoolf ρeoron on Ealdread (MS Eadread) daʒan. / 7 ne beo neann
mann swa deorif (MS ðeorif) þe hat (MS þehat) mið þ ic heobbe
ʒeʒyfene to hem, ne ʒhar brech seo ʒyrth ðρylc (MS ðyylc) Eorl
Syρard / 7 ic hebbe ʒetyðet hem ce frelyce (MS cefrelycc) sρa ænyʒ
mann leofand (MS leofanð) þeo ρelkynn ðeoronder (MS ðeorenðer).
7 loc hρylkun (MS hyylkun) byn þar / bydann (MS byðann) ʒeyld-
freo beo sρa ic byn 7 sρa ρillann ρallðeof 7 ρyʒande 7 ρyberth 7 ʒamell
7 kunyth 7 eallun mine / kynlinʒ 7 ρassenas. 7 ic ρille þ Thorfynn
heobbe soc 7 sac, toll 7 theam, ofer eallun þam landan on Carðeu
7 on / Combedeyfoch þ ρeoron ʒyfene Thore on Moryn daʒan freols
myd bode 7 ρytnesmann on þy ylk (MS þyylk) stop[1].

[1] The ends of MS. lines are marked by a *solidus* (/). The punctuation is added.

THE WRIT TRANSLATED

'Gospatrik greets all my dependants and every man free and *dreng*[1] who dwell in all the lands that were Cumbrian and all my kindred in friendly fashion. And I make known to you that my purpose is and (I am) perfectly agreeable that Thorfynn macThore be as free in all things that are mine in Allerdale [1] as any man be, either I or any (of) my dependants, in plain, in woodland, (or) in enclosure, in all things that are above the earth or thereunder, as far as Chalk [Beck, 8–9], as the Waver [30], as the Wampool [29–30], as Wiza Beck [31] and the plain at Caldbeck [275–81]. And I wish that the men abiding with Torfynn at Cardew and Cumdivock [in Dalston, 131 and 132] be as free in their persons as Melmor, Thore and Sygoolf were in Ea[l]dred's days. And let no man be so presumptuous as to withhold that which I have given to them, nor cause to be broken the guarantee of protection that Earl Syward and I have granted to them as freely as to any man living beneath the sky. And let everyone whosoever abiding there be as free of (royal) taxation as I am and as Walltheof and Wygande and Wyberth and Gamell and Kunith may wish, and all my kindred and dependants. And I wish that Thorfynn have *soc* and *sac*, *toll* and *team*, over all the lands at Cardew and Cumdivock that were given to Thore in Moryn's days free from the obligation to provide messengers (or, freely with the right to claim *bode* and witnessman) in that same place.'

---

[1] ON *drengr*, applied in Northumbria to a class of tenant who held by a tenure partly military and partly servile (EHR v, 625–32). It is preserved in the surname Dring and in Dringhoe (PN ERY 81), Dringsey Nook (PN Nt 208), etc. The spelling ðrenȝe may represent a genuine phonetic variant.

There are, at first glance, a number of suspicious features in the spelling and inflexional endings of the writ, and, if any plausible answer could be given to the question *Cui bono?* 'What is it in aid of?', one might be tempted to dismiss it as spurious. Yet neither Liebermann, on diplomatic grounds, nor Brandl, on the linguistic evidence, was prepared so to dismiss it, and it is easier, on balance, to accept it as a version—at more than one remove and sorely mangled in transmission—of a most uncommon document, an eleventh-century Northumbrian writ issued by a powerful subject. Otherwise one has to assume that it is a late—perhaps even a Tudor or Stuart—fabrication for the production of which no conceivable motive, such as the bolstering-up of some wildcat historical theory or the extension backward of a dubious pedigree, has been adduced.

Northumbrian history of the eleventh and twelfth centuries bristles with Gospatrics[1], and the identity of the issuer of this writ has, not unnaturally, been much debated. Greenwell, Ragg and Wilson argued for Gospatric son of Maldred (Earl of Northumberland 1067–72), and Liebermann concurred, partly, it may be, on the basis of the *Willelm* he believed to lie behind the *willann* of the manuscript. Yet it is not easy to be convinced that so well known a name as *Willelm* should have been corrupted in transmission, and it is more satisfactory to identify this Gospatric, as Davis did, with a son of the Uhtred who was Earl of Northumberland and was killed in 1016. This Gospatric, who was a maternal uncle of Gospatric son of Maldred, died himself in 1064.

The issuer of the writ does not style himself earl, though he is lord of Allerdale and Dalston, in the latter of which he describes himself as geld-free and is able to grant rights of jurisdiction (*soc 7 sac, toll 7 theam*). As he calls in Earl Siward of Northumbria to guarantee the *grith* he has granted to Thorfynn macThore, his tenant in Dalston, it is likely that he held that estate, and possibly Allerdale too, of the earl under whose vigorous rule many of "the lands that were Cumbrian" had been detached from their dependence on the King of Scots. The wording suggests that the earl was still alive when the writ was issued, and if that was the case it falls between c. 1041 and 1055, the years of Siward's tenure of the earldom of Northumbria.

[1] *Gwaspatric* is a British name meaning 'servant of (S.) Patrick.'

THE NORMAN PERIOD

Probably before 1066, and certainly by 1068, the area north of Derwent (or South Esk) and Eamont had been taken by the King of Scots, Simeon of Durham says "by violence." Though Malcolm III's representatives had sworn fealty for it to William I in 1068, in 1070 Malcolm invaded Yorkshire from the North-West, ravaging first Cleveland and Holderness and then Durham and Northumberland. William's counter-stroke came in 1072 when he advanced to the Tay and once again received homage for Cumbria. William determined none the less to establish the earldom of Richmond as a bulwark against invasion from the North-West. It is clear that the present county of Cumberland, barring the southern tip of Allerdale above Derwent, formed no part of the kingdom directly ruled by William, since only the area from the South Esk to Duddon Sands (the manor of *Hougun* held by Siward's successor Tostig in 1065 and later represented by the manor of Millom) was assessed in Domesday Book, and that as a part of Yorkshire. Gospatric II's son Dolfin, who governed from Carlisle in 1092, held the rest of the area as a man of the Scots king. This was not to William II's liking, and the *Anglo-Saxon Chronicle* (1092E) relates that "King William marched north to Carlisle with a large army, and re-established the fortress, and built the castle, and drove out Dolfin who had previously ruled the land there, and garrisoned the castle with his men, and afterwards returned to the south, and sent thither very many English peasants with wives and stock to dwell there to till the ground"; according to Henry of Huntingdon these settlers were "drawn from the south of England"— perhaps an inference from the wording of the *Chronicle*. Florence of Worcester adds "for this city, like some others in those parts, had been destroyed two hundred years earlier by the pagan Danes and had remained deserted up to this time." Malcolm not unreasonably regarded William's invasion as a breach of treaty agreement and when he could obtain no satisfaction invaded Northumberland, only to fall, with his eldest son Edward, in battle near Alnwick in 1093.

Immigration from the South at this time, or shortly after, is well illustrated by the occurrence of a fair number of names in *-by* to which a Norman, or at least a Continental Germanic, personal name is prefixed. The thickest concentration of these *-by* names is naturally in Carlisle and its immediate vicinity—Botcherby[1], Etterby, Harraby

---

[1] Cf. Botchergate in Carlisle (47).

and Upperby (43–4) with Rickerby[1] and Tarraby just across the
Eden in Stanwix parish (110) and outliers to the west in Wiggonby
(120) and to the east in Aglionby (158). Similarly there is a group
of three names of this type in Johnby (197), Ellonby and Lamonby
(240)—to the north-west of Greystoke Castle. It must be remembered
that the 'Normans' who came over with the Conqueror, or followed
in his wake, were not a homogeneous national body. Some of them
were Bretons such as the Alein and Wigan who gave their names to
Ellonby and Wiggonby, some of them Flemings such as the people
who gave their name to Flimby (286) or the individual Lambin after
whom Lamonby is called[2]. Names such as Corby (161), Dovenby
(284), Laconby (396), Melmerby (223), all of which contain a Goidelic
personal name, Maughonby (194), which has a British name, and
Allerby (306), Gutterby (380 and 448), Oughterby (143), all of which
have familiar Old English names, may be earlier, but it is just as
likely that some, or all, of them were given in the twelfth century[3].
Gamel, Orm and Ulf are such widespread Anglo-Scandinavian
names[4], Robert, Richard, Henry and John so common in the Norman
and early Angevin periods, that, cogent proof of identity being absent,
it would be hazardous to conjecture who gave his name to Gamelsby
(119), Hornsby (79) or Ousby (228), to Robberby (208), Rickerby
(110), Harraby (43) or Johnby (197). This is sometimes forthcoming.
We have good evidence that Gamblesby (192) and Glassonby (194)
derive their names from Gamel, son of Bern, and Glassam (*recte*
Glassan), son of Brictric, *drengs* of Henry I and the holders before
Hildred of Carlisle and his son Odard[5]. The Adam of Adamgill (422)
was certainly the Adam de Harrais of a grant to Holm Cultram,

[1] Cf. Rickergate in Carlisle (48).
[2] It may be useful to draw attention to the nomenclature of west Pembrokeshire, 'Little England beyond Wales' (which was largely given in the twelfth century and includes a much higher proportion of Continental Germanic names) though the corresponding second element there is -*ton*. See especially E. Laws, *The History of Little England beyond Wales* (London 1888), and B. G. Charles, *Non-Celtic Place-Names in Wales*, pp. xxxii and 1–108 (London 1938).
[3] A similar problem is presented by the -*bie* names of the adjoining county of Dumfriesshire (PN Dumf 3, 5, 6, 9, 13, 20, 24, 56, 92, 93).
[4] In Cumberland alone Gamel appears thrice, in the two names about to be cited and in *Gamelesflat* (242); Orm four times, in Hornsby (79), *Ormesby* (306) and *Ormescroft* (348 and 435); Ulf six times, in Uldale (327), Ullswater (36), Ousby (228), *Ulvescroft* (428), *vlueshouse* (457), and, almost certainly, in *Ulnescarthbec* (423).
[5] Glassonby illustrates well the racial complex in Cumberland. It is called after the Irish-named son of an English father. The names Birkby (282 and 424), Flimby (286), Ireby (299) and Scotby (163) provide further evidence, if it be needed.

c. 1225. Again there is a fair presumption that Rickerby (110) and Rickergate (48) derive their names from *Ricardus miles* who held Etterby in 1130 (P). He is apparently the *Ricard Ridere*[1] of the Book of Fees (1212), the predecessor (probably the grandfather) of Peter de Tilliol who held Etterby, Rickerby and a *baronia* in Rickergate (CW NS xxi, 139) and died in 1183. When less common names are involved one can with fair confidence point to an individual, asserting, for example, that the Etard of Etterby (43) once held the *terra que fuit Etardi* (1130P). Similarly it is difficult to avoid the conclusion that Willow Holme (43, *Holmus Werri* in 1201) derived its original name from the *Gueri Flandrensis* who held land and houses in Carlisle (1130P), or that the Nicholas who gave his name to Nicholforest (104) was Nicholas de Stuteville who held Liddesdale in John's reign. Again the *Ysac* of *Ysacby* (now Prior Hall in Low Ireby) was pretty certainly Isaac of Torpenhow (1165P), since Torpenhow is the next parish to Low Ireby (300). Again the eponym of Allerby (306) is probably the Ailward, son of Dolfin, of the Pipe Roll for 1163; of Farmanby (208) the Faremann of the Pipe Roll for 1170; of Ponsonby (426) the Puncon whose son John appears in the Pipe Roll for 1175; and of Aglionby the Walter Agullon who witnessed a charter to the monks of Wetheral c. 1130-1.

French names are borne by a couple of parishes, each with the element -*mont*. These are Beaumont (121)[2] and Egremont (379)[3], which latter is closely paralleled by Montacute (So). The same element is found in Grosmont (Mon, NCPNW 259), Mold (Flintshire, NCPNW 219-20), Mountsorrel (Lei) and Richmond (PN NRY 287), all great feudal castles set upon a hill. Belsay Fields (326), like Beaumont, are named from their fair site[4], Mopus[5] from the *malpas* 'evil passage' along the east side of Eskmeals Pool (347). Parsonby (310) and *Parsonthwait* (374) show the French *person* compounded with a Scandinavian word that had become part and parcel of the nomenclature of Cumberland. Also of French origin are Bailey (61), which was one of the divisions of Nicholforest, Barras

[1] *Ridere* is an English equivalent of *miles*, 'knight,' as in ASC 1090 E.
[2] Cf. PN La 177 and PN Ess 327.
[3] Cf. Egremont (Carmarthenshire, NCPNW 109).
[4] Cf. Belasis (Du, PN NbDu 16), Bellasis (Du, PN NbDu 16 and Nb, DEPN), Bellasize (PN ERY 245), Belsize Farm (PN Nth 232) and Belsize Park (PN Mx 112), to mention some parallels for which there is reasonably early evidence.
[5] Cf. Malpas (Ch, DEPN), Malpas (Co), Malpas (Mon, NCPNW 239). In the last case the name referred to the wet ground over which the old road had to travel.

found several times in the county, Farmery (338)[1], perhaps the infirmary of Calder Abbey, and Grune or Groyne (293) applied to a projection, artificially constructed or otherwise, which jutted into the sea and recalled a pig's snout. To these may be added the first element of Farmlands (422) and of Haltcliff (276), and the second of Crakeplace Hall (367), this latter being the French *place* in its sense of 'manor-house' (NED *sb.* 5 (*a*) and EDD *sb.* 3). The bishop's stronghold Rose Castle (134) was the flower of castles, and Ambrose Holme (160) contains, in a much distorted form and in a specifically English sense, the French *average*.

Manorial additions are exceedingly rare in Cumberland, the only surviving example of the normal type being Newton Reigny (227), which takes its difference from the family that held it in the twelfth and thirteenth centuries. In the sixteenth and seventeenth centuries, however, Nether Haresceugh (216) was called after the Charbocle family who held land in Kirkoswald in the fourteenth century[2]. In Randalinton (53) the christian name of a previous owner has been prefixed, in Hutton John and Hutton Roof (210) it has been added to an already existing place-name. The *Gamel* in *Clifton Gamel* (1212 Cur) has not survived (359). Crosscanonby (282) was the Crosby of the canons of Carlisle, Monk Foss (448) the foss of the monks of Furness Abbey, Priorsdale (175) the dale of the Prior of Hexham. In the sixteenth century the Armathwaite in Ainstable (168) was known as *Armathwayte Monialium* from the Benedictine nuns who have also left their name in Nunclose (206).

Fairly early in the twelfth century "the land of Carlisle," comprising modern Cumberland (less Allerdale above Derwent, Alston, the area between Esk and Sark, and almost certainly the north-east corner) and the barony of Appleby (now represented by the East and West Wards of Westmorland), were granted to Ranulf de Briquessart, styled le Meschin. Ranulf set up two baronies, Burgh by Sands to watch the Eden and Solway fords below Carlisle, and Liddel to defend the land approaches from Scotland. Burgh by Sands went to Robert de Trivers, to whom also was assigned the Forest of Cumberland, Liddel to Turgis Brundos[3]. Ranulf founded Wetheral and his

---

[1] Cf., too, *Fermery Hill* (348). These names do not necessarily belong to the twelfth century.

[2] Also *Sauser Salkild* was distinguished from King's Salkeld (237).

[3] If William Meschin were ever lord of Gilsland, as Camden's *Britannia* of 1637 (tr. Philemon Holland, p. 786) most improbably asserts, the latter was unable to dislodge Gille, son of Bueth, whose name is preserved in Gilsland, "the land that

brother William St Bees, both as cells of the great Benedictine Abbey of St Mary at York. On succeeding his nephew as Earl of Chester in 1120 Ranulf relinquished to Henry I "the land of Carlisle" of which he had never been more than *dominus*. Adding to it the barony of Kendal and Alston parish[1], the king divided the area into the sheriff-doms of *Chaerliolum* (not styled *Cumberland* till the Pipe Roll of 23 Henry II in 1177) and *Westmarieland*, and created several new baronies while keeping Carlisle itself and the Forest of Cumberland in his own hands. Allerdale (centre Cockermouth) went to Waldeve (Waltheof), son of Gospatric; after the district between Waver and Wampool had been split off to form a separate barony of Wigton it corresponded to the Ward of Allerdale below Derwent[2]. Greystoke (comprising the parish of that name and Dacre) was granted to Forni, and *Levington* (Kirklinton) to Richard de Boyville. It is interesting that two of these three grants should have been made to members of the pre-Conquest aristocracy[3]. The barony of Copeland, which may have been an earlier grant to William le Meschin, had not formed part of "the land of Carlisle," nor had the Sheriff of Cumberland authority therein till 1178. It was not included in the diocese of Carlisle, remaining, like Kendal and Kirkby Lonsdale, in the arch-deaconry of Richmond, which was in York diocese till 1541 and

---

Gille, son of Boet, held." It is more than doubtful if the English king's writ ran in Gilsland till the reign of Henry II, by whom Gilsland was granted to Hubert de Vaux, father of the Robert who held it in 1212. The Inquisition of Fees of 1212, most recently edited in *The Book of Fees commonly called Testa de Nevill* i, 197–200, provides most of the trustworthy information for feudal Cumberland in the days of Henry I.

For Turgis Brundos (or de Rossedale), who was still alive in 1158, see CW NS xxix, 49–56.

[1] Alston (171) belongs physiographically to Northumberland and remained ecclesiastically in the diocese of Durham (from which it passed to Newcastle on the division of the diocese in 1856), but Henry found it convenient to have the royal dues on the rich silver and lead mines collected by the Sheriff of Carlisle (CW viii, 21). In Alston the Northumberland *burn* prevails over the typically Cumberland *beck*.

[2] The (rural) deanery of Allerdale, in general corresponding to the Ward of Allerdale below Derwent, included as well the barony of Wigton—which suggests that the ecclesiastical organisation of the diocese of Carlisle was already in existence when the county was divided into wards. The remaining deaneries in Cumberland were those of Carlisle, which included most of Cumberland and Eskdale Wards, Cumberland, consisting chiefly of Leath Ward, and Copeland, which comprised Allerdale above Derwent Ward and formed part of the diocese of York and archdeaconry of Richmond; see C. M. L. Bouch, *Prelates and People of the Lake Counties*, pp. 136 ff. (Kendal 1948).

[3] In addition two of the sergeanties granted by Henry I were to men bearing the typically English names of Edmund and Edwin (*Book of Fees*, pp. 197–8).

Chester diocese from 1541 to 1856. It corresponded to the Ward of Allerdale above Derwent.

William II had apparently ordered the men of Carlisle to accept the jurisdiction of the Bishop of Durham, who had succeeded to the claims of his predecessor of Lindisfarne[1]. In spite of this John, who had been consecrated Bishop of Glasgow not later than 1117–18, was claiming and exercising episcopal rights in the district and at the same time kicking violently against the papal injunctions that bade him render obedience to York. The inconvenience of this to king and archbishop alike led Henry to have his chaplain Athelwulf, Prior of St Oswald's, Nostell, consecrated Bishop of Carlisle in 1133. His see was established at the Austin Priory of St Mary, which had been founded some time earlier in the reign, probably during the winter of 1122 when Henry paid a short visit to Carlisle[2]. The new diocese did not include Kirkandrews-upon-Esk (99), Upper Denton (81, in Durham till 1703), Alston (171), nor Copeland (*v. supra* p. xxxv); it did take in the barony of Appleby, the northern half of Westmorland.

Hardly was the see established when the troublesome reign of Stephen began. Athelwulf's diocese was occupied by the Scots, and in 1136 Stephen, to secure recognition of his claim to the English crown, granted the earldom of Carlisle to Henry, son of David I. The men of Carlisle fought on the Scots side at the Battle of the Standard; it was to Carlisle that Earl Henry fled after the defeat; and David I died there in 1153, predeceased by his son. From 1138 till his death in 1156 Athelwulf was in possession of his diocese, witnessing both the grant by which Earl Henry founded the Cistercian Abbey of Holm Cultram and David's confirmation thereof (1150)[3]. Other charters of David I and Earl Henry and confirmations by the father show that the Scots were firmly established in Carlisle and exercised effective control as far south as Copeland[4], or indeed the Ribble[5]. Most significant are two grants by David I. One is of a mark of silver annually from his mill of Scotby to the monks of Wetheral;

[1] VCH i, 302, declares that the documents "do not carry on the face of them the usual evidence of authenticity," but H. W. C. Davis does not stigmatise them (*Regesta* i, nos. 463 and 478), and there is no apparent reason why they should have been fabricated at Durham after the see of Carlisle had been established.

[2] See J. C. Dickinson, "The Origins of the Cathedral of Carlisle" (CW xlv, 134–43).

[3] Sir A. Lawrie, *Early Scottish Charters*, nos. CCXLIV and CCXLV.

[4] Lawrie, nos. CXXIII, CXXIV, CXXVI, CXL and CLXXXVII; this last is addressed "Omnibus probis hominibus suis Couplandie" and is executed at Lamplugh.

[5] W. Farrer, *Lancashire Pipe Rolls*, pp. 274–7.

this is addressed "Comitibus, justitiariis, totius Cumberlandiae, Francis et Anglis et Cumbrensibus," and is executed "apud Carliolum"[1]. The other is a grant of the eighth penny of his pleas in Cumbria to the see of Glasgow[2].

THE ANGEVIN PERIOD AND AFTER

Stephen's successor was a ruler of a very different stamp, and the Scots were not to hold "the land of Carlisle" much longer. In 1157 David's grandson Malcolm IV, a mere boy, was forced to give up the northern earldoms. The Scots did not as yet abandon hope of recovering Cumberland, for Carlisle, the great stronghold of royal power in the North-West, was besieged in 1173 and 1174, and again in 1215 when Cumberland was ravaged, not for the last time. It was only in 1242 that Alexander II finally relinquished his claim, receiving in compensation the manors of Penrith, Castle Sowerby, Langwathby, Salkeld, Carlatton and Scotby, all well within the English border. In 1296 began the wars of the Scottish Succession, and after that, even when there was peace between the two countries, the border could seldom be described as tranquil. Its fierce and hungry inhabitants preyed indifferently on Englishman and Scot, and by no means all the reivers who swung on Harraby Hill had come from the other side of the Kershope Burn. On *Hairibie* (Harraby), or elsewhere in Carlisle, suffered the famous outlaw whose name is preserved in Hobbie Noble's Well (63):

> Now Hobie he was an English man,
>   And born into Bewcastle dale,
> But his misdeeds they were sae great,
>   They banished him to Liddisdale (Child, no. 189).

Hobbie also appears in *Jock o' the Side* (Child, no. 187). Several forms have been taken from *Hobie Noble*, and that is not the only Border ballad that has been laid under contribution[3].

It should be noted that the peninsula between Esk and Sark was a neutral zone, the Debateable Land (38), that remained undivided till 1552 when the Scots Dyke was raised to mark the frontier between England and Scotland[4]. The area south of the Dyke, together with

---

[1] Lawrie, no. CXXIII of c. 1139.   [2] Lawrie, no. CXXVI of c. 1139–41.
[3] Most of those used describe events no earlier than the sixteenth century, but *Adam Bell, Clim of the Clough, and William of Cloudesly* (Child, no. 115) gives an impression of greater antiquity.
[4] On the D.L. see *Scottish Historical Review*, xxx, 109–25.

Nicholforest, was formed into the parish of Kirkandrews-upon-Esk by letters patent of 7 May 1631[1]; since 1552 it had apparently, like Nicholforest, been part of the parish of Arthuret[2].

Of the major names of the county the most recently bestowed is Maryport (305), called *Elmefoot* 'foot of the (River) Ellen' till the middle of the eighteenth century when Humphrey Senhouse gave his new port the name of his wife Mary. Senhouse Dock (285) and Senhouse St in Whitehaven (451) are also called after his family.

MINING AND PLACE-NAMES

The west coast of Cumberland south of the Ellen is now to a large extent industrialised, but the Whitehaven coalfield was little worked before the middle of the sixteenth century and is not reflected in early place-names. Iron ore (red hæmatite, mainly found in fissures of a narrow belt of Carbonaceous Limestone) is now chiefly mined in the Ehen valley (round Cleator and Egremont) and in Millom. These mines became really important about 1825, but it is known that they were already being worked in the Egremont district in the twelfth century[3]. Orgill 'ore valley' in Egremont (381) is recorded in the mid-fourteenth century, and with it may be taken *Orscarth* 'ore gap' in Birker and Austhwaite (344). A heap of charcoal gives its name to Burnbarrow field in Millom (420), and that is evidence for early smelting of iron ore. Furnace Beck (14), also in Millom, points the same way; it was so called in 1688. So also Cinderdale Beck (9), a tributary of the Irt, and Smithy Beck (27), which runs into Wast Water.

Lead was mined in different parts of the county. Brandelhow mine (372) is still shown by the 1″ map on the western shore of Derwent Water. From the twelfth century, if not much earlier, the most important source of lead (with some silver) was Alston (171 ff.)[4]. Here the lead-mining term *hush* 'artificial rush of water (to wash away surface soil)' is found on the 6″ map in Dowgang Hush and Redgroves Hush, *infra* 176–7. Dowkes (180) may be the plural of *dowk* 'tenacious black clay in a lead vein,' though the word can also mean 'broken mass of shale' (EDD).

[1] VCH ii, 117.   [2] CW OS viii, 289–306.
[3] Certainly before 1175, as can be seen from F. Grainger and W. G. Collingwood, *The Register and Records of Holm Cultram*, p. 21.
[4] The medieval mines of Alston are discussed in CW xlv, 22–33.

The *wad* 'graphite or plumbago,' from which the once famous Keswick lead-pencils were made, is recalled by *Woad holes* in Above Derwent (373); it was known as early as the reign of Henry VII.

Copper-mining has made a curious contribution to the place-names of the Borrowdale area, since the name Goldscope (370, Gottes Gab 'God's gift') was given by Daniel Hechstetter and the Germans who worked the rich veins of copper and lead for the Company Royal of Mines. This company was founded in 1564 and carried on till the royal monopoly was abolished by the Parliament some eighty years later. From Copperheap Bay (370), on the western shore of Derwent Water, the ore was boated to Keswick for refining at *the Smelthouses*, called *Schmaltzhüttin* by the German miners in 1569[1].

B. D.

---

[1] W. G. Collingwood, *Elizabethan Keswick*, p. 39. In the accounts of the German miners dealt with in that book there are some odd 'translations' of Cumberland place-names, as *Barnthal* for Borrowdale (349), *Farenseit* for Fornside (312), *Hiattmabainie* for Setmabanning (313), *Vorbarckh* for Fawepark (370). The Cumbrians had their revenge by turning the German surname Puchberger into *Puphparker*.

NOTES ON THE DIALECT OF CUMBERLAND
AS ILLUSTRATED IN ITS PLACE-NAMES

OE, ME, ON a usually remains, but some forms for names containing **braken** show a modern dialect variant [e].

OE, ON or ME a before nasals usually remains, but there are ME spellings with o in names containing **brame** (Branthwaite in Dean), **camb** (Black Comb), **land** (Gilsland, Kirkland parish, Kirkland in Blennerhasset, Sunderland) and **lang** (Longthwaite, Longtown). *Long-* is, of course, the most frequent modern form in names with **lang**, and *Comb* the only one from **camb**. Some names containing the elements listed have ME spellings in *au*, *aw* (Bramery, Brampton, the two Branthwaites, Kirkland parish) and *ou* (Branthwaite in Caldbeck, Black Comb).

OE, ON ā remains or was fronted in ME, and is spelt *a* except where the element has been Scandinavianised by influence of a corresponding ON word with -*ei*- (cf. Black Burn, Gatesgarth, Stainburn, Stainton). In early modern forms the sound is sometimes spelt *ay*, *ae*. In modern names it has developed either to [ei] as in Ameshaugh or to [iə] as in Smaithwaite, the names in Blea- from ON blá(r) and Wreay from ON (v)rá. Substitution of StEng rounded forms with o mostly dates from the sixteenth century. In Stonegarthside the spelling with o first appears in 1598, but the modern pronunciation has [ei]. OE āh, āg, āw and ON ág normally give ME and modern *aw*, as in Fawcettlees, but in Lodore, Low Ireby and some names with rāw StEng forms with *ow* have been substituted.

OE ăl before a consonant is frequently represented by **aw, au** in early modern forms. In the modern dialect it is pronounced [ɔ·] in some names (cf. Calva Hall, Calthwaite, Calvo, Salkeld, Walby), [ɔ] in some (cf. Caldbeck) and [ɔl] in some (cf. Aldby in Dacre and the spelling *Olby* for Auldby in 1765). In Fawepark the modern spelling represents the [ɔ·] pronunciation. Influence of the standard ModE *old* is perhaps found in the form *Oalby* (1697) for Aldby in Cleator.

OE æ is sometimes represented by ME e (as in Kershope, Hazelspring and some of the forms for Uzzicar) and sometimes by ME a.

OE ǣ usually gives e in ME, but the forms for names containing ON sætr show alternation between a and e in that element. There are ME spellings with *ee* and *ey, ei* for Seacote and Seaton, which contain OE sǣ.

OE, ME, ON e usually remains, but has been raised to i before [ŋ] in the words eng, flemyng(e), and Engla (cf. *Flashinge Dykes*, Skelling, Flimby, Inglewood).

OE ēa (monophthongised to ǣ) falls in with original ǣ and is usually represented by ME e. There are only *a* spellings for Kirkbampton and Shatton, in which names the vowel has been shortened. Eamont has ME *A-* and *E-*, and [iˑ] and [æ] are alternative modern pronunciations. þrēap- is spelt *Threip-* c. 1245 in the field-names of Gilcrux. In the modern pronunciation of some names (Sceugh Head, Ardale Head, Causewayhead) OE hēafod has developed to [hiˑd], without shortening of the vowel.

ME er is sometimes spelt ar from about the early thirteenth century onwards (Salter appears as *Saltargha* c. 1190, Hartside Height as *Hartishevede* c. 1200).

ME i is sometimes represented by e (cf. e.g. *Respholm*).

OE, ON ō usually gives [iu] in the modern dialect. The combination of ō with OE *h*, ON *g* is spelt *eu, ewgh, ugh, ew(e)*, occasionally in ME (cf. Hewthwaite Hall, Torpenhow, Haresceugh, Middlesceugh) and frequently in early ModE (cf. Heugh, Cleugh, Sceugh *passim* in minor names). For this development of ō in other combinations, for which spellings are somewhat later, cf. the early ModE spellings with *Mew* for Moota Hill and with *(e)u* for Nook in minor names. ME spellings with *u* for OE ō are rare.

OE, ON y usually falls in with i, and ȳ with ī, but there are very occasional ME spellings with *u* for earlier *y* (cf. Brigham, Kingbridge, Brig Stones, Brackenhill Tower, *Stubhill*, Salkeld, Millom). Preceded by r the sound sometimes becomes [u] as in *Rutterford*, Rudding.

The l in ME ol and ul was usually vocalised in the 16th century, as represented by names with *Pow* from poll, *Know* from cnoll. Cf. also Oulton, and the inverted spellings with -*l*- for Bowness.

OE ū occasionally remains, as in Souther Fell and Southerfield, Longtown (pronounced [lɔŋtuˑn]) and Abbey Cowper (pronounced [kuˑpə]).

OE -cg- is usually represented by -g-, as in Wigton and names containing hrycg. In names containing brycg StEng *bridge* has mostly been substituted.

OE final h or g, ON final g, are usually represented by modern [f], as in [brʌf] (Burgh by Sands), [skiuf] (Sceugh), [eimsha·f] (Ameshaugh), Barf in minor names (from be(o)rg).

The change of early ME hj to sh, noted in PN NRY and PN ERY, is found in Shoulthwaite.

Over-aspiration of OE hw, ON hv has resulted in numerous spellings with Qu-, cf. e.g. the forms for Whitehaven, Whitbeck, Whelpo, Cumwhitton and Whillimoor Foot. There are forms with Wh- from OE cw, ON kv, which suggest that in some ME dialects hw and cw had fallen together (v. PN ERY xxxi, Wheyrigg and Whirnestone in Egremont fields).

Metathesis of r is common; cf. e.g. the modern pronunciation of Burgh as [brʌf]: the forms showing this mostly date from the 16th century or later.

OE Sc- becomes Sk- owing to Scandinavian influence. Original c- from any source regularly gives modern [k].

There is confusion between initial f and th in Thornby, Fingland, Thursby, and of final f and th in Scarf (from skarð) in field-names. There appears to be confusion of th- with s- in Southwaite (earlier Thouthwaite) and Souther Gill [θʌtərgil], but both changes may be due to a desire to make the names more intelligible.

[ð] has become [d] in the common form Guard from garðr, and interchange of the two sounds is found in the forms for Warwick and Wetheral.

Initial [j] occasionally develops before a vowel; cf. Yanfold (Arthuret fields), The Oaks or Yakes (Upper Denton fields), Yak Hill (Skirwith fields) and the pronunciation [jæmen] for Eamont.

The northern ME ending -and of the present participle occurs in the forms for Rentland Burn, an alternative name being Hurlandwell (1603), and in Ratlandgill, 1568 in Caldbeck, Rutandpull, 1287 in Millom.

Names of which the first element is a personal name have usually no -s- to mark the genitive (the sign of the genitive, both singular and plural is generally omitted in north-country dialects when one noun qualifies another). There are numerous examples in the field-names quoted in the lists of personal names, infra 504. Cf. e.g. Lewinebrigg (c. 1210), Godbrigholm (c. 1280).

Traces of an inflexional -n- in early forms of place-names of which the first element is an adjective are very rare, but occur in those for Newton Reigny (Newinton' 1201) and Westnewton (Newenton 1360).

The forms occasionally show NCy t' for the: cf. e.g. *Twath head* 1731 for Wath Head.

It may be useful to note here that, apart from *The English Dialect Dictionary*, the most valuable works on the dialect of Cumberland are:

W. Dickinson, *A Glossary of the Words and Phrases pertaining to the Dialect of Cumberland*. London and Carlisle 1899.

E. W. Prevost, *A Supplement to the Glossary of the Dialect of Cumberland*. London and Carlisle 1905.

E. W. Prevost, *Second Supplement to the Glossary of the Dialect of Cumberland*. (Publications of the Philological Society, ix) 1924.

B. Brilioth, *A Grammar of the Dialect of Lorton (Cumberland) Historical and Descriptive*. (Publications of the Philological Society, i) 1913.

P. H. Reaney, *A Grammar of the Dialect of Penrith (Cumberland) Descriptive and Historical*. Manchester and London 1927.

BIBLIOGRAPHY AND ABBREVIATIONS

AA *Archæologia Æliana* (in progress).

Abbr *Placitorum Abbreviatio*, London 1811.

Acts Parl. Scot. *The Acts of the Parliaments of Scotland*, 12 vols., Edinburgh 1814–24, 1844, 1875.

AD *Catalogue of Ancient Deeds* (PRO) (1890 and in progress).

AllerA S. Jefferson, *The History and Antiquities of Allerdale Ward above Derwent*, Carlisle 1842.

AncPetitions Ancient Petitions (PRO).

AntIt *Itinerarium Antonini Augusti*, ed. G. Parthey and M. Pinder, 1848.

AOMB Augmentation Office Miscellaneous Books (PRO), vols. 376, 399, 405, 409, 414.

Arundel J. P. Yeatman, *The early genealogical history of the House of Arundel*, London 1882.

ASC *Anglo-Saxon Chronicle*.

Ass Assize Rolls (PRO): for Cumberland, nos. 130–43: for divers counties, nos. 1190, 1194, 1230, 1235, 1238–9, 1245, 1265, 1268, 1271, 1274, 1277, 1283, 1294, 1299, 1306, 1321, 1364, 1404, 1411a, 1417, 1424–5, 1426b, 1435, 1440, 1444, 1453, 1460, 1464, 1475, 1485, 1490, 1500, 1507, 1509, 1517, 1542, 1544, 1546.

AssNb *Three Early Assize Rolls for the County of Northumberland, sæc XIII* (Surtees Soc. 88), 1891.

Awntyrs off Arthure In *Scottish Alliterative Poems*, ed. F. J. Amours (Scottish Text Society), 1897: and unpublished thesis by A. G. Hooper in Leeds University Library.

Banco *Index of Placita de Banco* (PRO List and Indexes, no. 32), 1909.

BCS *Cartularium Saxonicum*, ed. W. de G. Birch, 3 vols., London 1885–93.

Bede *Historia Ecclesiastica*, ed. C. Plummer in *Venerabilis Baedae Opera Historica*, 2 vols., 1896.

Beds Bedfordshire.

BeethamRep W. Hutton, *Beetham Repository*, ed. J. Rawlinson Ford (CW, Tract Series 7), 1906.

Berks Berkshire.

Berw Berwickshire.

Björkman *v.* NP.

Bk Buckinghamshire.

Blome R. Blome, *A Generall Mapp of the Countie of Cumberland*, 1672.

BM *Index to the Charters and Rolls in the Department of Manuscripts, British Museum*, 2 vols., 1900–12.

BNB *Henricus de Bracton. Note Book*, ed. F. W. Maitland, London 1887.

BodlCh *Calendar of Charters and Rolls in the Bodleian Library*, ed. W. H. Turner and H. O. Coxe, Oxford 1878.

Boothby Documents in the possession of the Lady Henley, Lady Mary Murray and the late Lady Cecilia Roberts at Boothby.

Border	*Calendar of Letters and Papers relating to the affairs of the Borders of England and Scotland*, 2 vols., Edinburgh 1894–6.
Brayton	Documents in the possession of the late Camilla, Lady Lawson at Brayton.
Brisco	Documents in the possession of Captain A. Crofton of Brisco.
Bullock	H. Bullock, *Plan of the debateable lands on the borders, A.D. 1552*: in Nat.MSS.Scotland (q.v.), pt. 3, no. 37.
Burton, Antoninus	William Burton, *A commentary on Antoninus his Itinerary*, London 1658.
C	Cambridgeshire.
Cai	*Admissions to Gonville and Caius College*, ed. J. Venn and S. C. Venn, London 1887.
Caine	C. Caine, *A History of the Churches of the Rural Deanery of Whitehaven*, Whitehaven 1917.
CaineCl	C. Caine, *Cleator and Cleator Moor: Past and Present*, Kendal 1916.
Camden	W. Camden, *Britain*, translated Philemon Holland, 1610.
CantW	*Index of Wills proved in the Prerogative Court of Canterbury* (British Record Soc., in progress).
Card	Cardiganshire.
CarlCh	*The Royal Charters of Carlisle*, ed. R. S. Ferguson (CW, Extra Series x), 1894.
Carliol	*Register of John de Halton, Bishop of Carlisle, 1292–1324*, ed. W. N. Thompson (Canterbury and York Soc.), 2 vols., 1913.
Carliol	Registers of the Bishops of Carlisle (Diocesan Registry Office).
CartAnt	*The Cartae Antiquae Rolls 1–10*, ed. L. Landon (Pipe Roll Society, NS 17), 1939.
CCt	Court Rolls in the possession of the Dean and Chapter of Carlisle.
Celtic PN, Celtic PN Scot, C PNSc	W. J. Watson, *The History of the Celtic Place-Names of Scotland*, Edinburgh 1926.
Ch	*Calendar of Charter Rolls* (PRO), 6 vols., 1903–27.
Ch	Cheshire.
ChancP	*Calendars of the Proceedings in Chancery, in the reign of Queen Elizabeth*, 3 vols., 1827–32. *Index of Chancery Proceedings* (Series ii) (PRO Lists and Indexes, nos. 7, 24, 30).
ChancW	*Calendar of Chancery Warrants* (PRO) (in progress).
ChR	*Rotuli Chartarum*, 1837.
Chrest	J. Loth, *Chrestomathie bretonne*, Paris 1890.
Chrest, NSB	J. Loth, *Les noms des saints bretons*, Paris 1910.
ChronLaner	*Chronicon de Lanercost, 1201–1346* (Maitland Club), Edinburgh 1839.
Chron. Manniæ, Chronicle of Man	*Chronicon regum Manniæ, 1066–1266*: vol. iii of *Scriptores rerum Danicarum medii ævi*, 9 vols., Copenhagen 1772–1878.
Chron. Picts and Scots	*Chronicle of the Picts and Scots*, ed. W. F. Skene, Edinburgh 1867.
ChwAccts	Unpublished Churchwardens' Accounts.
CIL	*Inscriptiones Britanniae Latinae* (*Corpus inscriptionum Latinarum* vii), ed. AE. Hübner, Berlin 1873.
Cl	*Calendar of Close Rolls* (PRO) (in progress).
Clarke	J. Clarke, *A Survey of the Lakes of Cumberland, Westmorland and Lancashire*, 2nd ed., London 1789.

ClarkeM	Maps in Clarke (q.v.).
ClR	*Rotuli Litterarum Clausarum*, 2 vols., 1833–44.
Co	Cornwall.
Cocker	Documents in the possession of Lord Leconfield at Cockermouth Castle.
Cockersand	*The Chartulary of Cockersand Abbey* (Chetham Soc. New Series 38–40, 43, 56, 57, 64), 1898–1909.
CockersandA	Appendix to Cockersand (q.v.).
Coins	*Catalogue of English Coins in the British Museum, Anglo-Saxon Series*, 2 vols., 1887–93; *The Norman Kings*, 2 vols., 1916.
	Anglosachsiska Mynt, ed. B. E. Hildebrand, Stockholm 1881.
	English Coins, by G. C. Brooke, London 1950.
Cole	*Queen's Remembrancer Documents, thirteenth and fourteenth centuries*, ed. H. Cole (Rec.Comm.), 1844.
Coll. Top. et Gen.	J. G. Nichols, *Collectanea Topographica et Genealogica*, 8 vols., London 1834–43.
Corn	Cornish.
CP	Chancery Proceedings (PRO).
CR	Pipe Roll, Chancellor's Copy.
CRental	Rentals in the possession of the Dean and Chapter of Carlisle.
Ct	Court Rolls (PRO).
Cur	*Curia Regis Rolls* (PRO) (in progress).
CW	*Transactions of the Cumberland and Westmorland Antiquarian and Archaeological Society*, New Series (in progress).
CW(OS)	*Transactions of the Cumberland and Westmorland Antiquarian and Archaeological Society*, Old Series, 1866–1900.
D	Devon.
DandC	Documents in the possession of the Dean and Chapter of Carlisle.
DB	Domesday Book.
Db	Derbyshire.
Deed	Unprinted deed, copy of original at Langrigg Hall.
Denton	J. Denton, *An Accompt of the most considerable Estates and Families in the County of Cumberland*, ed. R. S. Ferguson (CW, Tract Series 2), 1887.
DentonA	Appendix to Denton (q.v.).
DentonL	Thomas Denton's Account of Cumberland and Westmorland 1687–8, compiled for Sir John Lowther (in the possession of the Earl of Lonsdale at Lowther Castle).
DepDu	*Depositions and other Ecclesiastical Proceedings from the Courts of Durham* (Surtees Soc. 21), 1845.
DEPN	E. Ekwall, *The Oxford Dictionary of English Place-Names*, 3rd ed., Oxford 1947.
Derwent	Documents relating to the estates of the Earls of Derwentwater in the possession of Greenwich Hospital (PRO).
Des	Descriptive field or minor name, discussed under that heading in the alphabetical list of elements.
Devonshire	Documents in the possession of the Duke of Devonshire at Carlisle.
DKR	*Reports by the Deputy Keeper of the Public Records.*
Donald	T. Donald, *The County of Cumberland Surveyed, 1770 and 1771* (engraved 1774 by J. Hodskinson), 1783.

Do	Dorset.
Du	Durham.
Dugd	W. Dugdale, *Monasticon Anglicanum*, 6 vols., 1817–30.
DuLa	*Calendar of Royal and other Charters printed in Appendices to the 31st, 35th and 36th Reports of the Deputy Keeper of the Public Records*, 1869–74.
DuLa	Duchy of Lancaster deeds (PRO).
Dumf	Dumfries.
DunBev	*Sanctuarium Dunelmense et Sanctuarium Beverlacense* (Surtees Soc. 5), 1837.
Earle	*Land Charters and Saxonic Documents*, ed. J. Earle, Oxford 1888.
EcclComm	Documents with the Ecclesiastical Commissioners.
ECP	*Early Chancery Proceedings* (PRO Lists and Indexes, nos. 1–10).
EDD	J. Wright, *The English Dialect Dictionary*, 6 vols., 1898–1905.
EETS	Early English Text Society.
EHN	O. S. Anderson, *The English Hundred-Names*, 3 vols., Lund 1934–9.
EHR	*English Historical Review* (in progress).
ElizKes	W. G. Collingwood, *Elizabethan Keswick* (CW, Tract Series 8), 1912.
Elvenavne	O. Rygh, *Norske Elvenavne*, Kristiania 1904.
EME	Early Middle English.
EnclA	Unpublished Enclosure Awards.
EPNS	English Place-Name Society (in progress).
ERY	East Riding of Yorkshire.
Eskdale	The Eskdale XXIV Book, Award of the Manor Court of Eskdale, Miterdale and Wasdalehead, 1587, copied in 1659. Late xviii-c. copy in the possession of Mrs Towers Hartley.
Ess	Essex.
ExchKR	Exchequer King's Remembrancer (PRO), vols. 37, 38, 42, 47.
ExonDB	Exeter copy of Domesday Book.
FA	*Feudal Aids* (PRO), 6 vols., 1899–1920.
Fan	Fanciful field or minor name, discussed under that heading in the alphabetical list of elements.
Fees	*The Book of Fees* (PRO), 3 vols., 1920–31.
Fetherstonhaugh	T. Fetherstonhaugh, *Our Cumberland Village*, Carlisle 1925.
Feudal Documents	*Feudal Documents from the Abbey of Bury St Edmunds*, ed. D. C. Douglas, London 1932.
FF	*Feet of Fines, t. Richard I to Edward IV* (CW vii). *Feet of Fines, Cumberland, during the reigns of Edward VI, Mary, Philip and Mary, and Elizabeth*, ed. J. P. Steel, London 1921.
FF	Feet of Fines (PRO).
Fine	*Calendar of Fine Rolls* (PRO) (in progress).
Fleming	Sir Daniel Fleming, of Rydal, *Description of the County of Cumberland, A.D. 1671*, ed. R. S. Ferguson (CW, Tract Series 3), 1889.
FlemingMem	*The Memoirs of Sir Daniel Fleming*, transcribed R. E. Porter, ed. W. G. Collingwood (CW, Tract Series 11), 1928.
FlemingMemA	Appendix to FlemingMem (q.v.).

For	Pleas of the Forest (PRO).
Fordun	*Johannis de Fordun Scotichronicon genuinum*, ed. T. Hearne, 5 vols., Oxford 1722.
Forssner	T. Forssner, *Continental-Germanic Personal Names in England*, Uppsala 1916.
Förster	M. Förster, *Keltisches Wortgut im Englischen*, Halle 1921; *Der Flussname Themse und seine Sippe*, München 1941.
Fountains	*Chartulary of Fountains Abbey*, ed. W. T. Lancaster, 2 vols., Leeds 1915.
FPD	*Feodarium Prioratus Dunelmensis* (Surtees Soc. 58), 1872.
Furness	*Furness Coucher Book* (Chetham Soc. 9, 11, 14, 74, 76, 78), 1886–7, 1915–16, 1919.
G	German.
G	C. and J. Greenwood, *Map of the County of Cumberland from an actual survey made in 1821 and 1822*, 1823.
Gaardnavne	*v.* NG.
GDR	Gaol Delivery Rolls (PRO), nos. 10a, 10b, 128, 132.
Gilpin	*Memoirs of Dr Richard Gilpin of Scaleby Castle*, ed. W. Jackson (CW, Extra Series ii), 1879.
Gilsland	*The Barony of Gilsland: Lord William Howard's Survey, taken in 1603*, ed. T. H. B. Graham (CW, Extra Series xvi), 1934.
Gl	Gloucestershire.
Glasgow	*Registrum Episcopatus Glasguensis* (Maitland Club), 2 vols., Edinburgh 1843.
GM	*The Gentleman's Magazine Library. English Topography*, pt. 2, London 1892.
Gospatric	Gospatric's writ, in the possession of the Earl of Lonsdale at Lowther Castle: *v.* Introduction, pp. xxvii ff.
Gough Map	*Facsimile of the ancient map of Great Britain in the Bodleian Library Oxford. A.D. 1325–50*, O.S., Southampton 1935.
Gray	*The Register, or Rolls, of Walter Gray, Lord Archbishop of York* (Surtees Soc. 56), 1872.
Gray	T. Gray, *Journal* (quoted in an appendix to West, q.v.).
Greenfield	*The Register of William Greenfield Lord Archbishop of York 1306–1315* (Surtees Soc. 145, 149, 151, 152, 153), 1931, 1934, 1936–8.
Gröhler	H. Gröhler, *Ursprung und Bedeutung der französischen Ortsnamen*, Heidelberg 1913–33.
Guisb	*Cartularium Prioratus de Gyseburne* (Surtees Soc. 86, 89), 1889, 1894.
H	W. Hutchinson, *The History of the County of Cumberland*, 2 vols., Carlisle 1794.
Ha	Hampshire.
Harrison	W. Harrison, *Description of Britain* in Holinshed's *Chronicles* (vol. i), 1577, 1586.
Harrison, *York Minster*	F. Harrison, *York Minster*, London 1927.
He	Herefordshire.
Herts	Hertfordshire.
Hesley	Transcripts provided by Miss Joan Wake of documents in the possession of the Charlton family at Hesleyside.
Hexham	*The Priory of Hexham* (Surtees Soc. 44, 46), 1864, 1865.

Heywood	John Heywood, *Woorkes. A dialogue conteyning prouerbes and epigrammes, 1562* (Spenser Soc.), 1867.
Hist.deS.Cuthberto	*v.* SD.
HMC	Historical Manuscripts Commission (in progress).
Hodskinson	*v.* Donald.
Hogan	E. Hogan, *Onomasticon Goedelicum locorum et tribuum Hiberniae et Scotiae*, Dublin 1910.
Holder	A. Holder, *Alt-Celtischer Sprachschatz*, 3 vols., Leipzig 1896–1907.
HolmC	F. Grainger and W. G. Collingwood, *Register and Records of Holm Cultram* (CW, Record or Chartulary Series vii), 1929.
HolmC	Holm Cultram Cartulary, copy in the possession of the Dean and Chapter of Carlisle.
HolmCA	Appendix to HolmC (q.v.).
Holyrood	*A Scottish Chronicle known as the Chronicle of Holyrood*, ed. M. O. Anderson, Edinburgh 1938.
Hosp	*Cartulaire général de l'ordre des hospitaliers de S. Jean de Jérusalem, 1100–1310*, ed. J. Delaville Le Roulx, 4 vols., Paris 1894–1906.
Hu	Huntingdonshire.
Hudleston	Documents in the possession of Mr F. Hudleston of Hutton John (forms transcribed by Mr C. Roy Hudleston, or, where indicated, by Miss J. Cameron).
Hutchinson	*v.* H.
Inq aqd	*Inquisitiones ad quod damnum*, 1803.
IOM	Isle of Man.
Ipm	*Calendar of Inquisitions post mortem* (PRO) (in progress).
IpmR	*Inquisitiones post mortem*, 4 vols., 1806–28.
IPN	*Introduction to the Survey of English Place-Names* (EPNS), 1923.
Jackson	W. Jackson, *Cumberland and Westmorland Papers and Pedigrees* (CW, Extra Series v and vi), 1892.
James	Documents in the possession of the late Mr W. A. James.
JohHex	*John of Hexham* (*v.* Hexham, vol. i).
K	Kent.
Kålund	P. E. K. Kålund, *Bidrag til en historisk-topografisk Beskrivelse af Island*, 2 vols., Copenhagen 1877–82.
KCD	*Codex Diplomaticus Aevi Saxonici*, ed. J. M. Kemble, 6 vols., 1839–48.
Kelly	*Kelly's Directory of Cumberland*, 1938.
Kendale	W. Farrer, *Records relating to the Barony of Kendale*, ed. J. F. Curwen (CW, Record or Chartulary Series iv, v and vi), 1923, 1924, 1926.
Kitchin	G. W. Kitchin, *Statesmen of West Cumberland*, 1904.
L	Lincolnshire.
La	Lancashire.
LaAss	*A Calendar of the Lancashire Assize Rolls* (Lancashire and Cheshire Record Soc. 47, 49), 1904, 1905.
LaCh	*Lancashire Pipe Rolls 1130–1216. Also Early Lancashire Charters.* Transcribed W. Farrer, Liverpool 1902.
Landnámabók	*Landnámabók*, Copenhagen 1900.
Laner	Lanercost Cartulary (18th century copy) in the possession of the Dean and Chapter of Carlisle.

LanerA   Deeds appended to *Laner* (q.v.).

Launceston   Cartulary of Launceston Priory (Lambeth Palace Library).

Laȝ   Laȝamon's *Brut*, ed. F. Madden, 3 vols., 1847.

Leath   S. Jefferson, *The History and Antiquities of Leath Ward*, Carlisle 1840.

Lei   Leicestershire.

Leland   J. Leland, *Itinerary*, ed. L. T. Smith, 5 vols., 1906–10.

Liber Landavensis   *The Text of the Book of Llan Dâv reproduced from the Gwysaney MS* by J. Gwenogvryn Evans, Oxford 1904.

Liddesdale   R. B. Armstrong, *A History of Liddesdale, Eskdale, Ewesdale, Wauchopdale and the Debateable Land*, pt. 1, *From the Twelfth Century to 1530*, Edinburgh 1883.

Lind   E. H. Lind, *Norsk-Isländska dopnamn och fingerade namn från medeltiden*, Uppsala 1905–15: *Supplementband*, Oslo 1931.

LindB   E. H. Lind, *Norsk-Isländska personbinamn från medeltiden*, Uppsala 1920–1.

Lindkvist   H. Lindkvist, *Middle-English Place-Names of Scandinavian Origin*, Uppsala 1912.

Lowther   Documents in the possession of the Earl of Lonsdale at Lowther Castle.

LowtherW   Documents in the possession of the Earl of Lonsdale at Whitehaven.

LP   *Letters and Papers Foreign and Domestic, Henry VIII* (PRO), 21 vols., 1864–1932.

LRMB   Land Revenue Miscellaneous Books (PRO), vols. 212, 213, 257, 258.

Lundgren   M. F. Lundgren and E. Brate, *Personnamn från medeltiden*, Stockholm 1892–1933.

Lysons   D. Lysons and S. Lysons, *Magna Britannia being A concise Topographical Account of the several counties of Great Britain, Volume the Fourth, containing Cumberland*, London, 1816.

M   R. Morden, *Cumberland* (map), 1695.

Mab   *The text of the Mabinogion...from the Red Book of Hergest*, ed. J. Rhys and J. Gwenogvryn Evans, Oxford 1887.

Machell   Manuscript collections for a history of Cumberland and Westmorland, written by the Rev. Thomas Machell c. 1690, now in the possession of the Dean and Chapter of Carlisle (6 vols.).

Mack   J. L. Mack, *The Border Line*, Edinburgh 1924.

Man.Roll   *The Manorial Roll of the Isle of Man* (*1511–15*), trans. T. Talbot, ed. G. F. Clucas, Oxford 1924.

Map   Unpublished maps.

MapC   Maps in Clarke (q.v.).

MapH   Maps in H (q.v.).

MapW   Maps in West (q.v.).

March   W. Nicolson (Bishop of Carlisle), *Leges Marchiarum*, Carlisle 1747.

Marstrander   C. J. S. Marstrander, "Det norske landnåm på Man" (*Norsk Tidskrift for sprogvidenskap* vi, 40–386).

McIntire   W. T. McIntire, *Guide to Carlisle and Neighbourhood*, Carlisle n.d.

ME	Middle English.
Med. Welsh	Medieval Welsh.
Mer	Merioneth.
MH	Documents in the possession of the Mounsey-Heysham family at Carlisle.
MHG	Middle High German.
Middle W	Middle Welsh.
MinAcct	Ministers' Accounts (PRO).
MIr	Middle Irish.
Misc	*Calendar of Inquisitions. Miscellaneous* (PRO) (in progress).
MLG	Middle Low German.
Mon	Monmouthshire.
Morden	*v.* M.
Moulton	H. R. Moulton, *Palaeography, genealogy and topography. 1930 catalogue*, Richmond 1937.
MNorw	Middle Norwegian.
ModW	Modern Welsh.
MS Harley	Harleian manuscripts (BM).
MSw	Middle Swedish.
MunRec	R. S. Ferguson and W. Nanson, *Some Municipal Records of the City of Carlisle* (CW, Extra Series iv), 1887.
Mx	Middlesex.
Nat.MSS Scotland	*Facsimiles of National Manuscripts of Scotland*, 3 pts. (O.S. Southampton), 1867–71.
Naworth	*The Household Books of Lord William Howard of Naworth Castle* (Surtees Soc. 68), 1877.
Naworth	Documents in the possession of the Earl of Carlisle at Naworth Castle.
NaworthA	Documents appended to Naworth (q.v.).
NB	J. Nicolson and R. Burn, *The History and Antiquities of the counties of Westmorland and Cumberland*, 2 vols., London 1777.
Nb	Northumberland.
NCPNW	B. G. Charles, *Non-Celtic Place-Names in Wales*, London 1938.
NCW	*North Country Wills* (Surtees Soc. 116, 121), 1908, 1912.
NCy	North Country.
n.d.	Undated.
NED	*New English Dictionary.*
Neilson	G. Neilson, *Annals of the Solway until A.D. 1307*, Glasgow 1899.
Nennius	*Historia Brittonum cum additamentis Nennii* (Mon. Germ. Hist. Auct. Antiquissm. Tomus xiii, pp. 111–222), 1898.
Netherby	Documents in the possession of Sir Fergus Graham of Netherby at Carlisle.
Netherhall	Documents in the possession of Lt.-Col. Guy Pocklington-Senhouse at Netherhall.
Nf	Norfolk.
NG	O. Rygh and others, *Norske Gaardnavne*, 19 vols., Kristiania 1897–1936.
NicVisit	W. Nicolson, *Miscellany Accounts of the Diocese of Carlisle with the Terriers etc. 1703–4*, ed. R. S. Ferguson (CW, Extra Series i), 1877.
NichVisit	
Norfolk	Documents in the possession of the Duke of Norfolk.
NorthReg	*Letters from Northern Registers* (Rolls Series), 1873.

NorthWe	J. F. Curwen, *The Later Records of North Westmorland* (CW, Record or Chartulary Series viii), 1932.
Norw	Norwegian.
NorwDial	Norwegian dialect.
NP	E. Björkman, *Nordische Personennamen in England*, Halle 1910.
NRY	North Riding of Yorkshire.
Nt	Nottinghamshire.
Nth	Northamptonshire.
O	Oxfordshire.
OAnglian	Old Anglian.
OBret, OBreton	Old Breton.
OBrit	Old British.
OCeltic	Old Celtic.
OCorn, OCornish	Old Cornish.
ODan	Old Danish.
OE	Old English.
OE Bede	*The Old English Version of Bede's Ecclesiastical History* (EETS 95–6, 110–11), 1890–8.
OFr	Old French.
OG, OGer	Old German.
Ogilby	J. Ogilby, *Itinerarium Angliae*, 1675.
OHG	Old High German.
OIr, OIrish	Old Irish.
OldW, OW, OWelsh	Old Welsh.
ON	Old Norse.
Orig	*Originalia Rolls*, 2 vols., 1805–10.
Orton	Orton Court Rolls in the possession of Captain Anthony Crofton.
O.S.	Ordnance Survey.
OSc, OScand	Old Scandinavian.
OSw	Old Swedish.
OWSc	Old West Scandinavian.
P	*Pipe Rolls* (Pipe Roll Society) (in progress).
(p)	personal name.
PaineBk	*A Paine Book for ye Hamlet of Weathermelocke* (in *The Parish Registers of Watermillock 1579–1812*, ed. H. Maclean, and *Matterdale 1634–1720*, transcribed H. Brierley, 1908).
Pap	*Calendar of Papal Registers* (PRO) (in progress).
Parker	C. A. Parker, *The Gosforth District: Its Antiquities and Places of Interest* (CW, Extra Series xv), 2nd ed. revised by W. G. Collingwood, 1904.
ParlSurv	Parliamentary Surveys (PRO).
Pat	*Calendar of Patent Rolls* (PRO) (in progress).
Patience	*Patience*, ed. Sir I. Gollancz, 2nd (revised) ed., London 1924.
PatR	*Rotuli Litterarum Patentium*, 1835.
PCC	*v.* CantW.
Pemb	Pembrokeshire.
Pipe	*The Pipe Rolls…for the Counties of Cumberland, Westmorland and Durham, during the reigns of Henry II, Richard I and John*, Newcastle 1847. *The Pipe Rolls of Cumberland and Westmorland 1222–1260*, ed. F. H. M. Parker (CW, Extra Series xii), 1905. *Great Roll of the Pipe for 26 Henry 3*, ed. H. L. Cannon, 1918.

PN BedsHu	*The Place-Names of Bedfordshire and Huntingdonshire* (EPNS), 1926.
PN Bk	*The Place-Names of Buckinghamshire* (EPNS), 1924.
PN C	*The Place-Names of Cambridgeshire and the Isle of Ely* (EPNS), 1943.
PN D	*The Place-Names of Devon* (EPNS), 2 vols., 1931–2.
PN Dumf	E. Johnson-Ferguson, *The Place-Names of Dumfriesshire*, Dumfries 1935.
PN ERY	*The Place-Names of the East Riding of Yorkshire* (EPNS), 1937.
PN Ess	*The Place-Names of Essex* (EPNS), 1935.
PN IOM, PN IOMan	*v.* PN Man.
PN La	E. Ekwall, *The Place-Names of Lancashire*, Manchester 1922.
PN Man	J. J. Kneen, *The Place-Names of the Isle of Man*, 6 vols., Douglas 1925–8.
PN Mx	*The Place-Names of Middlesex* (EPNS), 1942.
PN NbDu	A. Mawer, *The Place-Names of Northumberland and Durham*, Cambridge 1920.
PN NRY	*The Place-Names of the North Riding of Yorkshire* (EPNS), 1928.
PN Nt	*The Place-Names of Nottinghamshire* (EPNS), 1940.
PN Nth	*The Place-Names of Northamptonshire* (EPNS), 1933.
PN Sc, PN Scot	J. B. Johnston, *Place-Names of Scotland*, 3rd ed., 1934.
PN Shetland	J. Jakobsen, *The Place-Names of Shetland*, Copenhagen 1936.
PN Sr	*The Place-Names of Surrey* (EPNS), 1934.
PN SWY	A. Goodall, *Place-Names of South-West Yorkshire*, Cambridge 1914.
PN Sx	*The Place-Names of Sussex* (EPNS), 2 vols., 1929–30.
PN W	*The Place-Names of Wiltshire* (EPNS), 1939.
PN Wo	*The Place-Names of Worcestershire* (EPNS), 1927.
PN WRY	F. W. Moorman, *The Place-Names of the West Riding of Yorkshire*, Leeds 1910.
Pococke	*The travels through England of Dr Richard Pococke...during 1750,1751 and later years,* ed. J. J. Cartwright (Camden Soc. New Series 42, 44), 1888–9.
Polyolbion	M. Drayton, *Poly-Olbion*, 1612.
PR	Parish Registers (published).
PR	Parish Registers (unpublished).
Prevost	E. W. Prevost, *A supplement to the Glossary of the dialect of Cumberland* (by W. Dickinson), London 1905: second supplement (Philol. Soc. Publ. ix), 1924.
PrimW	Primitive Welsh.
PRO	Public Record Office.
Prompt Parv	*Promptorum parvulorum sive clericorum, Lexicon anglo-latinum princeps...A.D. c. 1440,* ed. A. Way (Camden Soc. Old Series 25, 54, 89), 1843, 1853, 1865.
Ptolemy	*Claudii Ptolemaei Geographia,* ed. C. Mullerus, Paris 1883.
QElizSch	P. H. Reaney, *Records of Queen Elizabeth Grammar School, Penrith* (CW, Tract Series 10), 1915.
Queen's	Documents in the possession of The Queen's College, Oxford.
QW	*Placita de Quo Warranto*, 1818.
R	Rutland.
RavGeog	*Ravennatis Anonymi Cosmographia,* ed. G. Parthey and M. Pinder, Berlin 1860.

Ray	John Ray, *A Collection of English Proverbs*, 2nd (enlarged) ed., Cambridge 1678.
RBE	*Red Book of the Exchequer* (Rolls Series), 3 vols., 1896.
R.C.Anc.Mon.Scot.Dumf.	*Royal Commission on the Ancient and Historical Monuments of Scotland, Dumfries*, Edinburgh 1920.
Redon Cart	*Cartulaire de l'Abbaye de Redon en Bretagne*, publié par M. Aurelien de Courson, Paris 1863.
REG	*v.* Glasgow.
RegDun	*Reginaldi Monachi Dunelmensis Libellus* (Surtees Soc. 1), 1835.
Rental	Unpublished Rentals (PRO).
RichWills	*Wills and Inventories from the Registry of the Archdeaconry of Richmond* (Surtees Soc. 26), 1853.
Ritchie, *St Baldred*	A. I. Ritchie, *The Churches of St Baldred: Auldhame, Whitekirk, Tyningham, Prestonkirk*, Edinburgh 1880.
RN	E. Ekwall, *English River-Names*, Oxford 1928.
Robinson	T. Robinson, *An Essay towards a Natural History of Westmorland and Cumberland*, London 1709.
Rose	J. Wilson, *Rose Castle, The Residential Seat of the Bishop of Carlisle*, Carlisle 1912.
Roxb	Roxburghshire.
Rygh GP	O. Rygh, *Gamle Personnavne i norske Stedsnavne*, Kristiania 1901.
S	C. Saxton, *Atlas of England and Wales*, 1576.
Sa	Shropshire.
Sanderson	Documents in the possession of Mrs Sanderson at Tunbridge Wells.
Sandford	E. Sandford, *A Cursory Relation of all the Antiquities & Familyes in Cumberland c. 1675*, ed. R. S. Ferguson (CW, Tract Series 4), 1890.
SandfordA	Appendix to Sandford (q.v.).
Sc	Scottish.
ScandCelts	E. Ekwall, *Scandinavians and Celts in the north-west of England*, Lund 1918.
Scandinavian Britain	W. G. Collingwood, *Scandinavian Britain*, London 1908.
Scotland	*Calendar of Documents relating to Scotland*, 4 vols., Edinburgh 1881–8.
SD	*Symeonis Monachi Opera Omnia: Historia Ecclesiae Dunhelmensis* (Rolls Series), 2 vols., 1882–5.
Sedgefield	W. J. Sedgefield, *The Place-Names of Cumberland and Westmorland*, Manchester 1915.
Sloane Roll	Sloane Collections (BM).
So	Somerset.
Speed	J. Speed, *The Theatre of the Empire of Great Britain*, 4 books, London 1611–12.
SP	State Papers Domestic (PRO).
SR	*Cumberland Lay Subsidy* (1332), ed. J. Steel, Kendal 1912.
Sr	Surrey.
St	Staffordshire.
Stainer	Forms supplied by Mr J. F. R. Stainer.
Star Chamber	*Proceedings in the Court of Star Chamber* (PRO Lists and Indexes, no. 13), 1901.
StB	*The Register of the Priory of St Bees* (Surtees Soc. 126), 1915.
StBA	Illustrative documents appended to StB (q.v.).

StEng	Standard English.
StJ	*Admissions to the College of St John the Evangelist*, parts i–iv, Cambridge 1882–1931.
StMaryY	*The Chronicle of St Mary's Abbey, York* (Surtees Soc. 148), 1934.
Studies[2]	E. Ekwall, *Studies on English Place-Names*, Stockholm 1936.
StudNP	*Studia Neophilologica*, Uppsala (in progress).
Survey	Unpublished Surveys (PRO).
Sx	Sussex.
Sykes	Forms supplied by the late Rev. W. S. Sykes.
TA	Unpublished Tithe Awards.
Tax	*Taxatio Ecclesiastica Angliae et Walliae*, 1802.
T.B.	Forms supplied by the late Mr T. Barnes.
Terrier	Terriers, published, chiefly in NicVisit (q.v.).
Terrier	Unpublished Terriers.
TestKarl	*Testamenta Karleolensia*, ed. R. S. Ferguson (CW, Extra Series ix), 1893.
Thomas	R. J. Thomas, *Enwau afonydd a nentydd Cymru*, vol. i, Cardiff 1938.
Thoresby	*Glossary of Yorkshire words from Thoresby's Letter to Ray April 27, 1703* (Ray's collection of words, English Dialect Society 1874).
Todd	H. Todd, *Account of the City and Diocese of Carlisle*, ed. R. S. Ferguson (CW, Tract Series 5), 1890.
Todd	An Account of Rentals, Surveys etc. of all lands in the possession of the Dean and Chapter of Carlisle by Dr Hugh Todd, 1686 (in the possession of the Dean and Chapter of Carlisle).
Trans. R.Hist.Soc.	*Transactions of the Royal Historical Society* (in progress).
Tullie	Documents at Tullie House, Carlisle.
VCH	*Victoria History of the Counties of England: Cumberland*, ed. J. Wilson, 2 vols., London 1901–5.
VE	*Valor Ecclesiasticus*, 6 vols., 1810–34.
Visit	*Visitations of the North* (Surtees Soc. 122, 123), 1912, 1921.
VitStC	*Two Lives of Saint Cuthbert*, ed. B. Colgrave, Cambridge 1940.
W	Welsh.
W	Wiltshire.
Watson	*v.* Celtic PN.
We	Westmorland.
Weekley	E. Weekley, *Surnames*, London 1916.
West	T. West, *A Guide to the Lakes in Cumberland, Westmorland and Lancashire*, 3rd ed., London 1784.
WestF	T. West, *The Antiquities of Furness*, Ulverston 1805.
Weth	*Register of the Priory of Wetherhal*, ed. J. E. Prescott (CW, Record or Chartulary Series i), 1897.
WethA	Appendix to Weth (q.v.).
W.G.C.	Forms and information supplied by the late W. G. Collingwood.
Whellan	T. Wright, J. G. Cumming, H. Martineau, *History and topography of Cumberland and Westmorland*, ed. W. Whellan, Pontefract 1860.
Whitehead	H. Whitehead, *Brampton in the Olden Times*, 1907.
Wickwane	*The Register of William Wickwane, Lord Archbishop of York 1279–1285* (Surtees Soc. 114), 1907.

Will	Unpublished wills.
Williamson	May G. Williamson, "The Non-Celtic Place-Names of the Scottish Border Counties" (thesis for Ph.D. degree in the University of Edinburgh Library).
WM	William of Malmesbury, *De gestis regum Anglorum* (Rolls Series), 2 vols., 1887–9.
Wo	Worcestershire.
Work	Documents in the possession of Mrs Chance at Workington Hall.
WRY	West Riding of Yorkshire.
Y	Yorkshire.
YCh	*Early Yorkshire Charters*, 8 vols.: vols. 1–3 ed. W. Farrer; vols. 4–8 ed. C. T. Clay; 1914–49.
Young	A. Young, *A six months tour through the north of England*, 4 vols., London, Salisbury and Edinburgh, 1770.
ZEN	E. Björkman, *Zur englischen Namenkunde*, Halle 1912.

PHONETIC SYMBOLS USED IN TRANSCRIPTION
OF PRONUNCIATIONS OF PLACE-NAMES

p	*p*ay	ʃ	*sh*one	tʃ	*ch*urch	ei	fl*ay*
b	*b*ay	ʒ	a*z*ure	dʒ	*j*udge	ɛ	Fr. jam*ai*s
t	*t*ea	θ	*th*in	aˑ	*fa*ther	ɛˑ	*the*re
d	*d*ay	ð	*th*en	au	c*ow*	i	p*i*t
k	*k*ey	j	*y*ou	a	Germ. m*a*nn	iˑ	f*ee*l
g	*g*o	χ	lo*ch* (Sc)	ai	fl*y*	ou	l*ow*
ʍ	*wh*en (Sc)	h	*h*is	æ	c*a*b	u	g*oo*d
w	*w*in	m	*m*an	ɔ	p*o*t	uˑ	r*u*le
f	*f*oe	n	*n*o	ɔˑ	s*aw*	ʌ	m*u*ch
v	*v*ote	ŋ	si*ng*	oi	*oi*l	ə	*e*v*e*r
s	*s*ay	r	*r*un	e	r*e*d	əˑ	b*ir*d
z	*z*one	l	*l*and				

Examples:

Edenhall [iˑdnəl], Sceugh [skiuf],
Mosedale [mouzdəl], Maughonby [maˑʍənbi].

NOTES

(1) The names are arranged topographically according to the Wards. Within each Ward the parishes are dealt with in alphabetical order, and within each parish the names of primary historical or etymological interest are arranged similarly, but in a number of parishes these are followed by one, or two, or three further groups of names. These groups, so far as they are represented, always appear in the following order: (i) minor names of topographical origin found largely in the second name of persons mentioned in early records dealing with the parish in question; (ii) names embodying some family name of Middle English or Early Modern English origin; (iii) minor names of obvious origin, or minor names for which we have only very late forms, about whose history it is unwise to speculate. All three types are represented under Dalston (135–7).

Street- and road-names are given in a note immediately following the interpretation of the parish name, e.g. the street-names of Whitehaven are given in a note at the end of the article on Whitehaven itself (451–2). The list of street-names in Carlisle is, however, given at the end of all the minor names in the Borough (46–9).

(2) Where a place-name is found only on the 6-inch O.S. map, this is indicated by putting 6″ after it in brackets, e.g. ‘Copt Hill (6″).’

(3) Place-names no longer current are marked as ‘(lost).’ This does not necessarily mean that the site to which the name was once applied is unknown. We are dealing primarily with names, and the names are lost. These names are printed in *italics* when referred to elsewhere in the volume.

(4) Place-names marked ‘(local)’ are not recorded on modern maps but are still current locally. ‘(field)’ after a name indicates that it is a field-name which has been dealt with separately, instead of among the section headed FIELD-NAMES at the end of the parish, because it is sufficiently interesting to warrant a full discussion.

(5) The local pronunciation of the place-name is given, wherever it is of interest, in phonetic script within square brackets, e.g. ‘Whelpo [ʍelpə]’ (278).

(6) Where a place-name element is printed in Clarendon type, e.g. ‘*v.* cokelayk,’ reference should be made to the discussion of that word in the alphabetical list of elements. *v.* ‘Des’ and *v.* ‘Fan’

indicate that the names in question are descriptive or fanciful terms discussed under those headings in the list of elements (468–9, 471–2).

(7) In the case of all forms for which reference has been made to unprinted authorities, that fact is indicated by printing the reference to the authority in *italic* instead of roman type, e.g. '1350 *Lowther*' denotes a form derived from a MS in contrast to '1673 CaineCl' which denotes one taken from a printed text.

(8) Where two dates are given, e.g. 'c. 1150 (c. 1225),' the first is the date at which the document purports to have been composed, the second is that of the copy which has come down to us.

(9) (p) after a place-name form indicates that the form occurred as a person's surname, not primarily as a reference to the place, as in the personal name *Hugh de Solum* (40) which contains the earliest form for the name of the lost hamlet of *Solum*.

(10) Where a letter in an early place-name form is placed within brackets, forms with and without that letter are found, e.g. '*Glassynby(e)*' means that forms *Glassynby* and *Glassynbye* are found.

(11) Where a place-name element is given with a letter bracketed, e.g. lē(a)h, w(i)elle, this indicates that the West Saxon and Anglian forms of the OE word differ, the bracketed letter being present only in the West Saxon form. The Anglian forms are, of course, the only ones found in the place-names of this county.

ADDENDA ET CORRIGENDA

ABBREVIATIONS. AB, *Analecta Bollandiana*. AngBbl, *Beiblatt zur Anglia*. AHR, *American Historical Review*. AntiqJ, *Antiquaries Journal*. Archiv, *Archiv für das Studium der Neueren Sprachen*. EngSt, *English Studies* (Amsterdam). JEGP, *Journal of English and Germanic Philology*. Literaturblatt, *Literaturblatt für germanische und romanische Philologie*. MLR, *Modern Language Review*. NoB, *Namn och Bygd*. NQ, *Notes and Queries*. RES, *Review of English Studies*. RevGerm, *Revue Germanique*. RevHist, *Revue Historique*. TLS, *The Times Literary Supplement*. YWES, *The Year's Work in English Studies*. ZONF, *Zeitschrift für Ortsnamenforschung*.

A.C.W. after a note indicates that the material was supplied by Mr A. C. Wood.

VOL I, PARTS I AND II

INTRODUCTION TO THE SURVEY AND THE CHIEF ELEMENTS IN ENGLISH PLACE-NAMES

Reviews of Vol. I, Parts I and II

MLR 21 (1926), 74–6, Bruce Dickins.
YWES 5 (1924), 55–65, J. R. R. Tolkien.
History 10 (1925–6), 157–9, L. V. D. Owen.
TLS 31 July 1924.
The Times 1 August 1924.
NQ 149 (1925), 197–8.
Literaturblatt 47 (1926), 15–19, H. M. Flasdieck.
Archiv 148 (1925), 297–8.
RevGerm 16 (1925), 208–9, F. Mossé.
RevHist 147 (1924), 283–4, Ch. Bémont.
AB 43 (1925), 170, P. Grosjean.
Part I, Chapter 4: NoB 12 (1924), 183–5, H. Lindkvist.
Part II: Archiv 149 (1926), 104–5, F. Liebermann.

Addenda et Corrigenda to Vol. I, Part II

p. 1, *s.v.* ærn. Delete 'Bruern (O).'

p. 3, *s.v.* ānstīg. For 'glossed as *termofilae*' read 'glossing *termofilae* (=Thermopylae)' (B.D., in MLR 21).

p. 4, *s.v.* bēan. Add 'Cf. Barton-in-Fabis (Nt) and Barton-in-the-Beans (Lei). With the latter may be compared Leland's *Itinerary* iv, 19: "Betwixt Trent ripe and Melton many benes and peson as yt is communely through al Leyrcestreshir"' (B.D. in MLR 21).

s.v. bearu. Add 'Barrow upon Humber (L) (*Adbaruae, id est Ad Nemus*, Bede, *Historia ecclesiastica*)' (B.D. in MLR 21).

For 'bēonet' read 'beonet.'

p. 10, *s.v.* būr. The word is used to mean 'lady's chamber' in ASC A s.a. 755 (B.D. in MLR 21).

p. 15, *s.v.* ceorl. Delete 'Chalgrave (O)' (*sic* for 'Chalgrove').

p. 19, for 'croh' read 'crōh.'

p. 22, *s.v.* dor. For 'Dorton (O)' read 'Dorton (Bk).'

p. 31, for 'hæþ' read 'hǣþ.'

p. 41, for 'ifig' read 'īfig.'

p. 50, for '*riþ, riþig*' read '*rīþ, rīðig.*'
p. 54, *s.v.* **spring**. For 'Hazelspring (O)' read 'Hazelspring (Cu).'
p. 56, for 'stigel' read 'stigel.'
p. 63, for 'wēala' read 'weala.'
p. 66, for 'wiðig' read 'wīðig.'

VOL. II

THE PLACE-NAMES OF BUCKINGHAMSHIRE

Reviews of Vol. II
  YWES 6 (1925), 48–50, J. R. R. Tolkien.
  History 11 (1926–7), 53–4, M. W. Hughes.
  TLS 27 August 1925.
  NQ 149 (1925), 305.
  Records of Buckinghamshire 11 (1920–6), 430–2.
  Literarisches Zentralblatt 76 (1925), 1743–4, J. W. Kindervater.
  RevGerm 18 (1927), 350–2, F. Mossé.
Vols. I and II
  MLN 42 (1927), 259–60, Kemp Malone.
  ZONF 4 (1928), 89–94, R. E. Zachrisson.
  EngSt 8 (1926), 153–6, J. Mansion.

Addenda et Corrigenda to Vol. II
  p. 43, *s.n.* LIMES END. For '1542 LP' read '1512 LP' (A.C.W.).
  p. 97, under IVINGHOE parish. Add 'CLIPPER DOWN is *Clyperdon* 1540 *MinAcct*,
Clyperden 1561 *Pat*' (A.C.W.).
  p. 195, *s.n.* MALLARD'S COURT. The derivation given is at variance with Wood
(*Parochial Collections*, ed. F. N. Davis, Oxfordshire Record Society), who calls it
Morley's Court now call'd Mallards Court, and mentions a brass inscribed to Robert
Morle, dated 1410, and another of the same name dated 1415.
  s.n. STUDDRIDGE. Add '*Stodrugge* 1254 FF.'
  s.n. WORMSLEY. Add '*Wudemundeslie* 1212 Fees (p).'
  p. 207, *s.n.* FASTENDICH. M. W. Hughes pointed out in *History* (1926) that the
name occurs elsewhere in the county. Scribbled on a leaf at the end of the Missenden
cartulary is a list of boundaries in which *Fastyngdich, ubi furcae sunt* occurs next to
Huntes Green, and may refer to the part of Grimsdike which crosses the road
between Missenden and Wendover.
  p. 250. For '*slæpe*' read '*slæp*' (J. R. R. Tolkien in YWES 6).
  p. 265. For 'Coster Pits, 112' read 'Coster Pits, 12.'

VOL. III

THE PLACE-NAMES OF BEDFORDSHIRE AND HUNTINGDONSHIRE

Reviews of Vol. III
  MLR 23 (1928), 353–4, P. H. Reaney.
  YWES 7 (1926), 36–8, Hilda M. Murray.
  History 12 (1927–8), 51–2, M. W. Hughes.
  RES 4 (1928), 366–8, J. H. G. Grattan.
  TLS 19 August 1926.
  NQ 151 (1926), 413–14.
  ZONF 5 (1929), 186–9, R. E. Zachrisson.
  EngSt 10 (1928), 11–14, J. Mansion.

Vols. I, II and III
    Englische Studien 62 (1927–8), 64–105, R. E. Zachrisson.
    AngBbl 38 (1927), 273–93, G. Binz.
Vols. II and III
    AHR 32 (1926–7), 302–3, Laurence M. Larson.
Addendum to Vol. III
    p. 224, *s.n.* BALDEWYNHO. Add 'The hamlet must have been near the boundary between Great Stukeley and Huntingdon, and the name survived as *Balmeshole* into the 19th century. Cf. VCH Hunts ii, 125: "In the 18th century the Town of Huntingdon began to assume the appearance it has at the present day. Originally it extended in length along the High Street from the bridge to a point called Balmeshole (Baldewyneshowa, Baudewenho, Bawynhoo, Bohn Holle, xii–xix century), where a small stream, now carried underground, crossed the road."'

VOL. IV

THE PLACE-NAMES OF WORCESTERSHIRE

Reviews of Vol. IV
    MLR 23 (1928), 481–3, P. Gurrey.
    YWES 8 (1927), 61–3, Hilda M. Murray.
    History 13 (1928–9), 46–7, M. W. Hughes.
    RES 4 (1928), 366–8, J. H. G. Grattan.
    Antiquity 2 (1928), 236–7, E. Weekley.
    TLS 29 September 1927.
    NQ 153 (1927), 215–16.
    AHR 33 (1927–8), 680, Laurence M. Larson.
    JEGP 28 (1929), 283–5, George T. Flom.
    EngSt 11 (1929), 24–7, J. Mansion.
    Studia Neophilologica 1 (1928), S. Karlström.
Vols. II, III and IV
    AB 46 (1928), 412–15, P. Grosjean.
Vols. III and IV
    RevHist 156 (1927), 350–1, Ch. Bémont.

Addenda et Corrigenda to Vol. IV
    We are indebted to Mr E. F. Gray for the following notes.
    p. 159, *s.n.* RYALL. Add 'RYALL HILL appears as *Royal Hill* on some old maps and in *TA*.'
    p. 160, *s.n.* STRATFORD. This is referred to as *Staltinge or Stratford Ford* in a survey of 1647, which might be a bungled attempt to record some name indicating that the ford carried the saltway over Ripple Brook.
    Under RIPPLE parish. Add 'FOWLERS COPY FARM is to be associated with Thomas *Fowler*, who held several properties in 1664 (*CourtR*). THE GROVE is *Riall Grove* 1593 WillsP. *The Grove* 1805 *TA*. HOME FM is locally called *the Buildings Farm* as it is largely built from remains of the former Rectory Tithe Barn, damaged by fire c. 1850, and a stockyard from paving stones from an adjacent Roman road.'
    p. 168, *s.n.* STONEBOW. Add 'Bow BRIDGE in Ripple is *Bowbrydge* 1589 *CourtR*, *Stone-bridge* 1675 Ogilby, and has on one side a long stone parapet in the form of a bow.'
    p. 272, under OMBERSLEY parish. Add 'TURN MILL is *Tirmill* 1540 *MinAcct*' (A.C.W.).

VOL. V
The Place-Names of the North Riding of Yorkshire

Reviews of Vol. V
 MLR 25 (1930), 195–6, O. K. Schram.
 YWES 9 (1928), 51–3, Daisy E. Martin Clarke.
 Antiquity 3 (1929), 373–7, R. E. Zachrisson.
 The Times 10 August 1928.
 NQ 155 (1928), 377.
 AHR 34 (1928–9), 635–6, Laurence M. Larson.
 RevHist 160 (1929), 91–2, Ch. Bémont.
 EngSt 12 (1930), 188–90, J. Mansion.
Vols. IV and V
 ZONF 7 (1931), 248–57, S. Karlström.
 AngBbl 42 (1931), 325–9, G. Binz.

Addenda et Corrigenda to Vol. V
 p. xxxix, l. 14. For '*Anglicanum*' read '*Anglicum*.' l. 42. For '*Englische*' read '*Englischen*' (O.K.S. in MLR 25).
 p. 19, under SUTTON ON THE FOREST parish. Add 'THRUSH HOUSE is *Thrushouse* 1543 LP, cf. *Thrushes Close* ib.' (A.C.W.).
 p. 29, under MARTON LE FOREST parish. Add 'SPELLAR HO, SPELLOW. Cf. *Spellohill* 1536 *MinAcct*. Apparently 'speech hill,' but the place is not near the site suggested on p. 8 for the meeting place of the Wapentake.' (Form supplied by A.C.W.)
 p. 32, under SHERIFF HUTTON parish. Add 'FOSS HO is *le Fosse house* 1536 *MinAcct*' (A.C.W.).
 p. 45, under NEW MALTON. Add 'NOTE. CASTLEGATE, MARKET PLACE, NEWBIGGIN, OLD MALTONGATE and YORKERSGATE are *Castle Gate* (v. gata), *Merketstede* (v. stede), *Newbiginge Gate* (v. bigging, gata), *Oldmarton Gate* and *Yarkehouse Gate* 1540 *MinAcct*' (A.C.W.).
 p. 84, under MARISHES. Add 'DEERHOLME GRANGE takes name from *Dereham* 1540 *MinAcct*' (A.C.W.).
 p. 126, under WHITBY. Add 'NOTE. BAGDALE, BAXTERGATE and GRAPE LANE are *Bag(e)dale*, *Bax(s)tergate* and *Grapelane* 1540 Whitby: for the last v. PN ERY 289.' (Forms from A.C.W.)
 p. 141, under LOFTUS parish. Add 'ROSE CROFT is *Rossecrofte* uncertain date Guis, *Roscroft* 1540 Guis' (A.C.W.).
 p. 202, under ARDEN. Add 'BREWSTER HILL is so named 1536 *MinAcct*. HARKER YATES is *Hartay* (? *Harcay*) *Yates* 1536 *MinAcct*' (A.C.W.).
 p. 281, under GREAT SMEATON. Add 'THORPE ROW FM takes name from *Thorprawe* 1539 LP' (A.C.W.).
 p. 294, under MARRICK. Add 'COLT PARK WOOD takes name from *Colte Parke* 1540 *MinAcct*' (A.C.W.).
 p. 321. *Cēolfrið* should not be starred (O.K.S. in MLR 25).

VOLS. VI AND VII
The Place-Names of Sussex, Parts I and II

Reviews of Vols. VI and VII
 YWES 10 (1929), 61–4, Daisy E. Martin Clarke.
 History 16 (1931–2), 343–5, A. E. Levett.

RES 7 (1931), 459–62, P. Gurrey.
TLS 1 May 1930.
The Times 29 April 1930.
NQ 158 (1930), 287–8.
AngBbl 42 (1931), 205–7, W. Preusler.
EngSt 13 (1931), 200–1, J. Mansion.
AB 49 (1931), 186–8, P. Grosjean.
RevGerm 22 (1931), 196–7, F. Mossé.
Part 1: Sussex County Magazine 4 (1930), 100–2, Alfred Anscombe. Sussex Notes and Queries 3 (1930–1), 32–4.
Part 2: Sussex Notes and Queries 3 (1930–1), 65–7.

Addenda to Vol. VI
The material for the following addenda was supplied by Mr W. H. D. Riley-Smith from deeds in his possession.
p. 103, *s.n.* BUSHETTS. Add '*Byshoppes* 1780.'
p. 120, *s.n.* COOMBE BOTTOM. Add 'cf. *Combottom coppice* 1780'; *s.n.* HARWOODS GREEN. Add 'cf. *Harwoods coppice or Harwoods Piece* 1780.'
p. 135. After 'NEWPOUND COMMON' add '(so named in 1882).'
p. 136, *s.n.* BALDWIN'S HANGER add '*Baldwins Hanger* 1838'; *s.n.* BREWHURST FM add '*Bruers als. Bruars* (messuage and watermill) 1554, *Brewers, Brewers Mill* 1615, *Bruhurst* 1641.'
p. 158, last paragraph. Add 'HYES is *Hyesse* c. 1537, *Huighes Meade* 1610, *Hyes* 1639, Highes 1756.'

VOLS. VIII AND IX

THE PLACE-NAMES OF DEVON, PARTS I AND II

Reviews of Vols. VIII and IX
YWES 12 (1931), Mary S. Serjeantson.
History 18 (1933–4), 39–41, J. E. A. Jolliffe.
RES 9 (1933), 365–7, P. H. Reaney.
TLS 12 May 1932.
The Times 6 May 1932.
Devon and Cornwall Notes and Queries 18 (1934–5), 126–7, J. J. Alexander.
EngSt 15 (1933), 184–5, J. Mansion.
NoB 21 (1933), 162–7, E. Tengstrand.
Part 1: Devon and Cornwall Notes and Queries 17 (1932–3), 68–74, E. S. Chalk. AngBbl 46 (1935), 233–4, F. Holthausen.
Part 2: AngBbl 46 (1935), 294–5, F. Holthausen.

Addenda et Corrigenda to Vols. VIII and IX
C.S. after a note indicates that the material was supplied by Mr Cecil Spiegel-halter. *Barum*=unpublished Barnstaple Borough Records in the North Devon Athenæum.
p. 21, *s.n.* EXETER. Sir William Craigie has drawn our attention to the apparent occurrence of *Esses* as an abbreviated form of *Excestre* in the following verse of the Anglo-Norman *Vie de Thomas Becket* by Beneit, composed in 1184:

> Il enveiad bien tost apres
> Vn arcevesque mult engres
> Dan Rogier,
> Celuy d'Everwic, e celuy de Esses,
> Autres evesques e clers ades
> Sey escuser.

These were the messengers sent by King Henry to the Pope, and among the bishops who are mentioned in the Latin life is Bartholomæus Exoniensis episcopus.

p. 26, Barnstaple street-names. *s.n.* BARBECAN RD add '*Le Barbigan* 1329–30'; *s.n.* BEAR ST add '*Barstret* 1311–12'; *s.n.* CASTLE ST add '*Castel lane* 1317–18, *Castelstrete* 1325–6'; *s.n.* CROCK ST (now CROSS ST) add '*Crocstrete, Crokstrete* 1344–5'; *s.n.* HOLLAND ST add '*Holondestret* 1322–3'; *s.n.* JOY ST add 'The eastern end is still called Eastgate from *la Estyete* 1331–2'; *s.n.* PAIGES LANE add '*Pageslane* 1423–4, Mr Spiegelhalter says it runs behind the houses in High St and was used by servants'; *s.n.* SOUTH ST add 'Cf. Thomas atta *Southyete* 1319–20'; *s.n.* STRAND add '*Strandam Barnestapol* 1312–13'; *s.n.* WELLS ST add '*Wilstrete* 1359–60'; *s.n.* ANKER LANE add '*Oncrelane* 1311–12, *Onkerelane* 1314–15, first element "recluse," this is the early name of Market St.' To the names discussed in this article can be added PULCHRASS ST, which is *Pulkars* 1347–8, *Pulcars* 1397–8. These forms were supplied by C.S. from original documents, mostly in the North Devon Athenæum.

p. 27, *s.n.* NEWPORT add '*Nyweport Episcopi* 1352 *Barum*'; *s.n.* GORWELL add '*Gorwell* 1378 *Barum* (p)'; *s.n.* RUMSAM add '*Rumesham* 1269 Exmoor (p)'; these forms are all from C.S. Mr Spiegelhalter also informs us that the Barum document referred to under Sticklepath and Ettiford on the same page should be dated c. 1309 not c. 1280.

p. 29, *s.n.* FROGMORE PLANTATION add '*Vroggemere* 1331'; *s.n.* NARRACOTT add '*Northecote* 1293'; *s.n.* UPCOTT add '*Uppecote* 1301.' These forms were supplied by C.S. from Bittadon deeds.

p. 31, *s.n.* HUNNACOTT add '*Honicote, Honnecote* 1319 *Barum* (p)'; *s.n.* LEWORTHY add '*Leuaworth* 1318 *Barum* (p)' (C.S.).

p. 32, *s.n.* BRAUNTON add the form *Braunton Abbas* 1367 *Barum*, from the Abbot of Cleve; *s.n.* FAIRLINCH add '*Fairesling* 1167 P (p), *Fayrelinch* 1323 *Barum* (p)' (C.S.).

p. 34, *s.n.* PIPPACOTT. Add '*Pippecote* 1303 *Barum* (p)' (C.S.).

p. 35, *s.n.* LEARY BARTON. Add '*Lairy, Layri* 1310 Exon (p)' (C.S.).

p. 36, *s.n.* GUBBS. Add 'Nich. *Gubbe* (1476 *Barum*)' (C.S.).

p. 37, *s.n.* ASHELFORD. Add '*Assiliswrth* 1240 *Barum* (p)' (C.S.).

p. 40, *s.n.* CRACKAWAY. Add '*Crakeweie* 1219 *Ass*' (C.S.).

p. 55, under PILTON parish. Add 'CLADAVIN was probably the home of Sarra de *Clodefenne* (1332 *SR*), v. fenn' (C.S.).

p. 57, under ARLINGTON parish. Add 'BESSHILL was probably the home of Wm. de *Bezill* (1272 ChR)' (C.S.).

p. 60, *s.n.* SLOCOMBESLADE add '*Sloucom* 1303 *Barum* (p)'; *s.n.* WATERLET LINHAY add '*Waterlete* 1327 *Barum* (p)' (C.S.).

p. 62, *s.n.* SHUTSCOMBE. Add '*Scottescombe* 1319 *Barum* (p)' (C.S.).

p. 67, *s.n.* TUCKINGMILL. The surname *Tokynmil* (1332 *SR*), noted by Mr Spiegelhalter, contains an earlier example of this name: the first example of the term in NED is dated 1467–8.

p. 71, *s.n.* SNACKSLAND. Cf. Thomas *Snak* (1423 Totnes) (C.S.).

p. 75, under HARTLAND parish. Add 'MANSLEY CLIFF takes name from *Manselegh* 1383 Pat: possibly "*Man's* wood or clearing," v. lē(a)h.' (Form from A.C.W.)

p. 84, *s.n.* PUSEHILL. C.S. notes the surname *Puue* (1167 P), probably another example of the surname discussed here.

p. 88, *s.n.* OLDISCLEAVE add '*Hodesclive* 1167 P (p)'; *s.n.* WOODVILLE COTTAGES add '*Woodwille* 1326 FF (p)' (C.S.).

p. 96, *s.n.* PUTSHOLE. C.S. notes the surname *Pyet* (1349 Exon), i.e. 'magpie,' from which this place-name may be derived.

p. 105, *s.n.* BOWDEN. Add '*Bugedon* 1219 *Ass*' (C.S.).

p. 106, *s.n.* LITTLE MARLAND. C.S. notes that the surname *Pye* does occur in Devon in medieval records.

p. 110, *s.n.* FRIZENHAM. C.S. notes that *Frise, Frisa, Frysa* occur as surnames in medieval records for the county.

p. 114, *s.n.* GRABBISHAW. C.S. notes that there are many occurrences of this surname (*Grob, Grobi, Grubbi, Grubbe, Grobbe*) in Devon in the 13th and 14th centuries. *s.n.* BRYNSWORTHY add '*Brendewrd*' 1195 P, *Brundesworthi* 1219 *Ass*': the second form is from C.S.

p. 118, *s.n.* SCOTTINGTON BARTON. Wm. *Scotenaton* is mentioned 1332 *SR* (C.S.).

p. 120, *s.n.* PEAGHAM BARTON. Add '*Pageham* 1260 Exon (p)' (C.S.).

p. 128, *s.n.* MOORHAY. A surname *Morhay, Moray, Morehay* occurs 1324 Exon and 1332 *SR* (C.S.).

p. 149, *s.n.* GREYLAND. Cf. Wm. *Greylond*, mentioned 1332 *SR* (C.S.).

p. 162, *s.n.* VOLEHOUSE. Cf. the surnames *Phugelhus* 1219 *Ass* and *de Fogelhous* 1332 *SR* (C.S.).

p. 163, *s.n.* PARNACOTT. C.S. draws attention to the surname *Pern* (1313 Exon) and the modern name *Pearn*.

p. 164, *s.n.* PINSLOW. Add '*Penteslo* 1238 *Ass* (p), *Pentelow* 1312 Exon (p)' (C.S.).

p. 165, *s.n.* CORSCOMBE. Add '*Cockescom* 1219 *Ass* (p)' (C.S.).

p. 179, *s.n.* BRIDGE PARK. Add '*Brusshe parke* 1540 *MinAcct*' (A.C.W.).

p. 180, under BROADWOODWIDGER parish. Add 'HOLE is so named 1540 *MinAcct*, *v.* holh.' (Form from A.C.W.)

p. 188, *s.n.* WADDLESTONE. C.S. informs us this is now pronounced [wa'sɔn].

p. 196, *s.n.* PRINCE HALL. C.S. draws attention to the surname *Prinne* 1238 *Ass*, *Prin* 1372 Exon.

p. 214, *s.n.* MONKSTONE. A much earlier form is *Munekestune* c. 1171 Reports and Transactions of the Devonshire Association lxxv, 257. 'Monk's tūn.'

p. 219, *s.n.* PIXON LANE. Add '*Piggesdone* 1318 Exon (p), *Pygysdone* 1388 Exon (p)' (C.S.). Mr Spiegelhalter also draws attention to the surname *le Pig* 1238 *Ass*, *le Pigh* 1284 FA.

p. 226, *s.n.* CUXTON. Add '*Cokeston* 1238 *Ass* (p)' (C.S.).

p. 233, *s.n.* GER TOR. C.S. suggests that the surname *atte Gorde* mentioned 1332 *SR* indicates that the first element of this name may be topographical.

p. 259, *s.n.* FAUNSTONE. The modern pronunciation is [vænstoun], and the surname Vanstone is derived from the place-name (C.S.).

p. 263, *s.n.* PITTEN. Add '*West Putte* 1219 *Ass*' (C.S.).

p. 272, *s.n.* ERMINGTON. Add the form *Irminton* 1219 *Ass* (C.S.).

p. 301, *s.n.* COOMBE. Add 'Cf. Juliana in the *Comb* 1332 *SR*' (C.S.).

p. 302, *s.n.* BENJIE TOR. Add 'Cf. Rd. de *Bengiu* 1275 RH' (C.S.).

p. 306, *s.n.* HAZELWOOD. Add '*Halswood, Hasylwood* 1538 LP' (A.C.W.).

p. 318, *s.n.* SIGDON. Add '*Siggedon* 1219 *Ass*' (C.S.).

p. 330, *s.n.* BLACKLAND. Add 'R. *Blakelond*, mentioned 1332 *SR*, may derive his surname from this place-name' (C.S.).

p. 345, *s.n.* HOLDRIDGE. Add '*Hiallerig* 1219 *Ass*' (C.S.).

p. 352, *s.n.* KEWSLAND. C.S. informs us that the surname *le Keu* 'the Cook' occurs very often in Devon from 1238 (*Ass*) to 1765.

p. 362, *s.n.* PARTRIDGE WALLS. Wm. *Pertrych* is mentioned 1419 Exon (C.S.)

p. 371, *s.n.* LARKSWORTHY. The Rev. H. Fulford Williams informs us that John Larkworthy of Larkworthy married Johanna Kelly of North Tawton in 1593. Mr Williams has also supplied the following notes on names in North Tawton parish. THE BARRACKS (recently changed to Exeter St) was so named from its being the location of a French prisoners-of-war camp in the 18th century and up to 1815.

BOUCHIER'S HILL (often corrupted to Butcher's Hill) is named from Sir William *Bouchier* (14th and 15th centuries). COTTELL'S BARTON is named from the *Cottell* family who held the lands and built the house 1562–1672. FARLEY'S CROSS (O.S.) was formerly *Farley's Grave*, named from a poacher called Robert Farley, buried at the cross roads here after committing suicide c. 1830. LAKEWAY leads to a stream.

p. 375, *s.n.* BURSTON. C.S. notes that the family name *B(o)urdeville* occurs 1212 FF, 1332 *SR*, 1336 FF and in a number of later sources, all relating to this county.

p. 394, *s.n.* STONELAND. C.S. says this is *Steniland* 1219 *Ass*.

p. 412, *s.n.* BREMBRIDGE. Add '*Bremerigg* 1219 *Ass*' (C.S., ex. inf. J. P. Benson).

p. 420, *s.n.* RAMSTORLAND. C.S. suggests that the surname *Hammescurt*, mentioned 1293 Fees, is a misreading of *Rammesturt*, and thus an earlier reference to this place.

p. 469, *s.n.* CHALLABROOK. Add '*Cherlebrok* 1332 *SR* (p)' (C.S.).

p. 516, *s.n.* OCCOMBE add '*Okcomb* 1332 *SR* (p)'; *s.n.* STRINGLAND add '*Strange-land* 1219 *Ass*' (C.S.).

p. 519, *s.n.* APPAWAY. Add '*Appawa* 1238 *Ass* (p)' (C.S.).

p. 521, *s.n.* CADDAFORD. Add '*Cadeford* 1332 *SR* (p)' (C.S.).

p. 526, *s.n.* CHALLAMOOR. Add '*Chuldemore* 1332 *SR* (p)' (C.S.).

pp. 531–2, *s.n.* SPARKHAYNE. Rt. *Sparke* is mentioned 1238 *Ass* (C.S.)

p. 537, *s.n.* UFFCULME. Mr Eric E. Barker draws attention to the form *Offaculum* n.d. (1247) in Hearne's *John of Glastonbury*, pp. 375–8.

p. 551, *s.n.* WHITEDOWN. Add '*Whytedowne* 1552 Pat' (A.C.W.).

p. 557, *s.n.* WATERLETOWN. Add 'This was probably the home of Peter atte *Waterlegh*, mentioned 1332 *SR*' (C.S.).

p. 562, *s.n.* HALSEWOOD. Add '*Alswod* 1238 *Ass* (p)' (C.S.).

p. 578, *s.n.* BLAMPIN FARM. Emma *Blauncpayn* is mentioned 1332 *SR* (C.S.).

p. 613, *s.n.* ALMSHAYNE FM. Add 'Cf. Saher teutonicus 1215 Exon, John Alman 1381 Exon' (C.S.).

p. 616, *s.n.* CULM DAVY. Mr Eric E. Barker draws attention to the form *Cumbe juxta Culum* c. 760 (1247) in Hearne's *John of Glastonbury*, pp. 370–5.

p. 621, *s.n.* ROCKENHAYNE. C.S. suggests that *Hokeneheyne* 1332 *SR* (p) refers to this place.

p. 634, *s.n.* CUTHAYS. Delete *Cuittehege*, which is an error for *Cnitte-*, and refers to Knightshayne Fm on p. 652 (*Cniteheya* 1219 *Ass*).

p. 647, *s.n.* BUCEHAYES. C.S. suggests that the first element is the surname *Buz*, *Beuz*, found in medieval records. The form quoted in the text probably does not belong here, v. PN Mx, p. xxxi.

p. 649, under UPLYME parish. Add 'WOOLCOMBE FM. Cf. *Wullacomb Wood* 1544 LP' (A.C.W.).

p. 666. For '*hylte' read 'hylte.'

VOL. X

THE PLACE-NAMES OF NORTHAMPTONSHIRE

Reviews of Vol. X

YWES 14 (1933), 59–60, Mary S. Serjeantson.
History 19 (1934–5), 54–5, F. M. Powicke.
TLS 20 April 1933 [B.D.].
The Times 11 April 1933.
AngBbl 49 (1938), 353–4, F. Holthausen.
RevGerm 25 (1934), 38–9, F. Mossé.
EngSt 17 (1935), 147–8, J. Mansion.

Vols. VI–X
 ZONF 10 (1934), 243–51, R. E. Zachrisson.
Vols. VIII–X
 AB 51 (1933), 421–3, P. Grosjean.
Vols. I–X
 RevHist 173 (1934), 393–400, Ch. Bémont.

Addenda et Corrigenda to Vol. X
 p. 85, *s.n.* HEYFORD. Mr I. B. Terrett calls our attention to the form *altera Haiford* in DB.
 p. 145, *s.n.* COURTEENHALL. The form *alio Cortenhalo* also appears in DB, though there does not appear to be any other evidence that there were two settlements here (I. B. Terrett).
 p. 148, *s.n.* NUN MILLS. Add '*Quengeens Milles* 1539 *MinAcct*' (A.C.W.).
 p. 157, *s.n.* BRITAIN SALE. Mr G. E. Glazier, the County Librarian of Bedfordshire, has drawn our attention to the following quotation from G. J. Turner's *Select Pleas of the Forest*, Selden Society xiii, 48, which suggests that the meaning given in EDD for *sale* in Nth goes back at least to the 13th century: "Presentum est per eosdem et conuictum quod cum dominus rex precepisset quod placea illa in qua facta fuit uendicio in parco de Ridelinton' includeretur ut posset recrescere Petrus de Neuill' fecit agistare quam plurima animalia in placea illa postquam inclusa fuit que corroserunt sciones cipporum quercum uenditarum et subbosci prostrati et magnam partem eorum cipporum fecit eradicare et carbonare ita quod nunquam recrescet ad dampnum domini regis et heredum suorum de centum libris vnde idem Petrus respondeat...."
 The quotation refers to Ridlington R, and Mr Glazier informs us that there is also an Old Sale Wood in Braunston R, within the bounds of the medieval Forest of Rutland. The *vendicio* in this passage evidently involved the oaks, probably in addition to the underwood (cf. Fair Oak Sale on p. 205).
 p. 174, *s.n.* WELDON. Little Weldon is *parva Weledone* 1086 DB (I. B. Terrett).
 p. 185, *s.n.* NORTHALL. Add '*Northall* 1542 *MinAcct*' (A.C.W.). This does not support the etymology suggested in the text.
 p. 235, under EYE parish. Add 'RUMPHREY'S BALK. Dr E. T. Leeds has called our attention to a probable early occurrence of this name in Walter of Whittlesey's *Historia Coenobii Burgensis* (*Historiæ Anglicanæ Scriptores Varii*, ed. J. Sparke, 1723, p. 154). Godfrey of Croyland (Abbot 1299–1321) is said to have been responsible for some building work "apud Rumpele prope Eyebiri." *v.* lē(a)h; the first element is uncertain.'

VOL. XI

THE PLACE-NAMES OF SURREY

Reviews of Vol. XI
 YWES 15 (1934), 43–4, Mary S. Serjeantson.
 AntiqJ 14 (1934), 437–40.
 Antiquity 9 (1935), 371–3, Wilfrid Bonser.
 TLS 24 May 1934 [B.D.].
 The Times 15 May 1934.
 RevHist 173 (1934), 630–1, Ch. Bémont.
 EngSt 18 (1936), 261–3, J. Mansion.
Vols. X and XI
 RES 11 (1935), 246–8, P. H. Reaney.

Addenda et Corrigenda to Vol. XI

p. 35, *s.n.* TOOTING. Mr F. J. Randell Creasy informs us that over fifty years ago there was a large round mound (encircled by a ditch), probably twenty or thirty feet high, to the north of Tooting Bec Road. Nearby were some fields called Totterdown Fields, on which the L.C.C. carried out one of their first housing schemes. *Totterdown* could represent OE *tōtærn-dūn, 'hill with a watch tower'; and 'people of the look out place' may therefore be the better etymology for Tooting.

p. 83, under WALTON-ON-THE-HILL parish. Add 'FRITH PARK takes name from *Fryth*, *le Fryght* 1506 *Ipm*, v. fyrhþ(e).' (Forms from A.C.W.)

p. 182, *s.n.* TONGHAM. The Rev. T. F. Griffith informs us that the "small tributary stream" of the Wey mentioned in this article is topographically impossible and at the present time only ditches carry off water towards the Blackwater.

pp. 222–3, *s.n.* FASTBRIDGE. The first element of the lost names *Berdespich*, which are found in Sr and K, and of the possibly identical Barsbeck in Holland (*Berspijck* 1363) might be an unrecorded mutated form of OE *bord* 'board,' cf. ON *byrði*. This word is the most satisfactory explanation which can be offered for the first element of the name of Beard Mill in Stanton Harcourt O (*Berdemulne* early 13th, *Burdemulne* 1278–9, *Berdedmille* 1375). The names discussed in PN Sr might thus mean 'causeway of planks in marshy land.'

VOL. XII

THE PLACE-NAMES OF ESSEX

Reviews of Vol. XII

YWES 16 (1935), 57–8, C. L. Wrenn.

RES 15 (1939), 119–21, G. V. Smithers.

AntiqJ 15 (1935), 485–7.

Antiquity 10 (1936), 114–15, Frank B. Jessup.

TLS 30 May 1935 [B.D.].

The Times 11 June 1935.

The Essex Review 44 (1935), 262–4.

RevHist 177 (1936), 453–5, Ch. Bémont.

Vols. XI and XII

AB 53 (1935), 444–6, Ch. Bémont.

Addenda et Corrigenda to Vol. XII

p. 14, *s.n.* HALFWAY REACH. Mr A. C. Hart informs us that according to Perry's map of Dagenham Breach, which appeared in his book of 1721, Halfway House was on the opposite bank of the Thames from Dagenham. The tree itself was in Dagenham.

p. 43, *s.n.* FRYERS. Add '*Freers* in Hatfyld, parcel of the possessions of St Bartholomew Spyttyl in London 1542 LP Addenda' (A.C.W.).

p. 109, *s.n.* SNARESBROOK. For 'EAS vii' read 'EAS viii.'

p. 212, *s.n.* REDWARD. A much earlier form is *le Redewerde* 1387 *Ipm* (A.C.W.). This is clearly another occurrence of the word **werþ* 'marsh,' discussed under Labworth (148). The first element might be 'reed.'

p. 223, under PURLEIGH parish. Add 'SOUTH HOUSE (6″) is *Southhous* 1396 *Ipm*' (A.C.W.).

p. 246, *s.n.* COVAL HALL. This might be named from Geoffrey *Colvyle* of Chelmsford, mentioned 1421 *FF* (A.C.W.).

p. 265, foot-note 4. Add '*Mounteneys* 1390 Cl' (A.C.W.).

p. 280, foot-note 2. Add '*Morehall in Wrytele* 1376 *FF*' (A.C.W.).
p. 456, foot-note 7. Add '*Nicholes* 1382 Cl' (A.C.W.).
p. 474, *s.n.* DUNMOW. Add the form *Muchdunmo* 1546 (C. Welch, *Register of Freemen of the City of London*, London 1908, p. 84): cf. Much Hadham PN Herts 176–7.
p. 495. MERKS HALL is probably *Merkestenement* 1349 Cl (A.C.W.).
p. 497, *s.n.* MONK ST. Add '*Monkstrete* 1384 *FF*' (A.C.W.).

VOL. XIII

THE PLACE-NAMES OF WARWICKSHIRE

Reviews of Vol. XIII
 YWES 17 (1936), 47, C. L. Wrenn.
 RES 14 (1938), 373–4, P. H. Reaney.
 AntiqJ 16 (1936), 475–6.
 Antiquity 11 (1937), 240–2, Wilfrid Bonser.
 TLS 4 July 1936 [B.D.].
 The Times 14 July 1936.
 AHR 43 (1937–8), 928–9, W. Notestein.
 AngBbl 50 (1939), 33–4, F. Holthausen.
 AB 55 (1937), 146–7, P. Grosjean.
 RevHist 180 (1937), 158, Ch. Bémont (review reprinted 182 (1938), 181).
Vols. XI–XIII
 History 22 (1937–8), 348–50, F. M. Powicke.
 The New England Quarterly 10 (1937), 400–1, F. P. Magoun, Jr.
Addenda et Corrigenda to Vol. XIII
 p. 8, under ROAD-NAMES. Add 'Dr T. Loveday informs us that THE IDWAYS occurs as a field-name at Arlescote in the parish of Warmington, the fields so called lying on a track to Nadbury Camp. This is clearly another example of OE *þēod-weg* 'via publica,' discussed PN BedsHu 122. In Beds it survives as Ede Way, by the common process of misdivision in which *Th-* was taken for the definite article.'
 p. 9, *s.n.* MEREWAYS. For 'Tamworth' read 'Tanworth.'
 p. 51, under SUTTON COLDFIELD parish, *s.n.* BEGGARS BUSH. Add 'In a Boundary Dispute Award of 1802 (Wa County Records) this appears some two miles from its present position.'
 Add 'BOLDMERE is *Bowmere* 1802 *Warwickshire County Records, Baldmoor* 1840 *EnclAMap.*' We owe the above information to Mr M. W. Beresford.
 p. 185, *s.n.* WESTLEY BRIDGE. Mr B. W. Johnson informs us that it is Westley Bridge which carries the road from Stoneleigh to Gibbet Hill, and the bridge a mile to the east, known locally as Finham Bridge, carries the old direct road from Coventry to Warwick.
 p. 291, under PACKWOOD parish. Add 'HOCKLEY HEATH is *Hokeley Heth* 1540 *MinAcct*' (A.C.W.).

VOL. XIV

THE PLACE-NAMES OF THE EAST RIDING OF YORKSHIRE AND YORK

Reviews of Vol. XIV
 MLR 33 (1938), 424–5, Gunnar Knudsen.
 YWES 18 (1937), 46, C. L. Wrenn.

RES 16 (1940), 246–7, P. H. Reaney.
History 23 (1938–9), 158–60, David Douglas.
Medium Ævum 8 (1939), 233–5, G. L. Brook.
TLS 18 December 1937.
NQ 174 (1938), 17–18.
AngBbl 50 (1939), 134–5, F. Holthausen.
AB 56 (1938), 177, P. Grosjean.

Addenda to Vol. XIV

p. 46, *s.n.* BENNINGHOLME GRANGE. Add '*graungie de Benyngholme* 1542 *MinAcct*' (A.C.W.).
p. 206, *s.v.* NOTE. Add 'HALLGATE is *Hallegate* 1536 *MinAcct, v.* gata' (A.C.W.).
p. 224, *s.n.* OXMARDIKE. Add '*Oxmerdyk* 1358 *Pat*' (A.C.W.).

VOL. XV
THE PLACE-NAMES OF HERTFORDSHIRE

Reviews of Vol. XV

MLR 35 (1940), 74–5, A. Macdonald.
YWES 19 (1938), 35–6, Marjorie Daunt.
History 24 (1939–40), 172–3, David Douglas.
Antiquity 12 (1938), 432–6, O. G. S. Crawford.
TLS 12 November 1938 [B.D.].
The Times 9 September 1938.
NQ 175 (1938), 143–4.
East Herts Archæological Society Transactions 10 (1937–9), 238–40.
AngBbl 50 (1939), 4–5, F. Holthausen.
Neophilologus 25 (1940), 68–9.

Addendum et Corrigendum to Vol. XV

p. 199, foot-note 6. Add '*Doos* 1373 Cl' (A.C.W.).
p. 315, *s.v.* cock sb¹. The page reference should be '72' not '22.'

VOL. XVI
THE PLACE-NAMES OF WILTSHIRE

Reviews of Vol. XVI

MLR 35 (1940), 223–6, Dorothy Whitelock.
RES 17 (1941), 246–7, P. H. Reaney.
History 24 (1939–40), 363–4, David Douglas.
Antiquity 15 (1941), 33–44, H. C. Brentnall.
TLS 29 July 1939 [B.D.].
The Times 29 July 1939.
NQ 177 (1939), 70–2.
The Wiltshire Archæological and Natural History Magazine 49 (1940–2), 130–2.

Vols. XV and XVI

AB 59 (1941), 326–7, P. Grosjean.

Addenda et Corrigenda to Vol. XVI

p. xxxiv, last line. For '95' read '94.'

p. 24, *s.n.* HANNINGTON. Mr Eric E. Barker draws attention to the forms *Hanandone* t. Alfred, Edgar, Ethelred II (1247) in Hearne's *John of Glastonbury* 370–5, and *Hanandune* t. Ethelred II in William of Malmesbury's *de Antiquitate Glastoniensis Ecclesiae* printed by Hearne, *Adam of Domerham*, vol. i.

p. 28, foot-note 3. Add '*Warnefordes Place* 1541 LP' (A.C.W.).

p. 52, *s.n.* DANIELS WELL. Add '*Danyell Well* 1540 *MinAcct*' (A.C.W.).

p. 90, *s.n.* Cokestrete. Add '(*Cook Street* is said in a Turnpike Act of 1767–8 to be part of the route of the London Road through Chippenham).'

p. 135, *s.n.* LONDON BRIDGE. Add 'Cf. *London Bridge Lane* 1767–8 Turnpike Act.' This and the preceding note were supplied by Mr A. Cossons.

p. 150, *s.n.* CHALFORD. This may be *Chardeforde* 1543 LP (A.C.W.). The first element of the early name could be *ceart*, found once in a field-name in W (426).

p. 174, *s.n.* MONKTON DEVERILL. Mr Eric E. Barker draws attention to the forms *Vuerdeverel* c. 930 (1247) in Hearne's *John of Glastonbury*, pp. 370–5, and *Werdeverel, hoc est, Munecatone* c. 930 (c. 1130) in William of Malmesbury's *de Antiquitate Glastoniensis Ecclesiae*. The prefix is probably 'over.'

p. 259, foot-note 3. Add '*Haylle* c. 1260–70 Hist. MSS Commission, Various Collections iv, p. 100' (A.C.W.).

p. 301, *s.n.* MILDENHALL. Mr Eric E. Barker draws attention to the form *Mildenhealh* c. 775 (1247) in Hearne's *John of Glastonbury*, pp. 370–5.

p. 342, *s.n.* MANKHORN ROUND. Add '*Mangcorne Fild* 1528 AD.'

p. 407, *s.v.* feld. Add 'Clanville.'

p. 415, under CELTIC NAMES A. Add 'Croucheston (?)' (D.W. in MLR 35).

p. 468, *s.n.* Mill Ham in BREMHILL. Add '*Milham* 1540 *MinAcct*' (A.C.W.).

p. 476, *s.n.* Dewpit in MELKSHAM add '*Dup'te* 1540 *MinAcct*' (A.C.W.); *s.n.* Barelegs in MELKSHAM add '(*Berlegges* 1540 *MinAcct*)' (A.C.W.).

p. 493, *s.n.* Newlands in CALNE. Add '*Nywelond* 1282, *Nyvvelonde* 1316, *Niewelond* 1328, *Niewelonde* 1335 Hist. MSS Commission, Various Collections iv, pp. 103, 105, 106, 107' (A.C.W.).

p. 495, *s.n.* Wood Leaze in HILMARTON add '*Woodleese* 1539 *MinAcct*' (A.C.W.); *s.n.* Worrells in LYNEHAM add '*Litle Wyralles, Brodewyralles* 1539 *MinAcct*' (A.C.W.); *s.n.* Pucklechurch in LYNEHAM add '(cf. *Poculchurchmede* 1529 *MinAcct*)' (A.C.W.).

VOL. XVII

THE PLACE-NAMES OF NOTTINGHAMSHIRE

Reviews of Vol. XVII
MLR 37 (1942), 81–3, Dorothy Whitelock.
History 26 (1941–2), 85–6, David Douglas.
AntiqJ 21 (1941), 351–2, F. W. Jessup.
TLS 3 August 1940 [B.D.].
NQ 179 (1940), 197–8.
Vols. XVI and XVII
YWES 21 (1940), 25, Dorothy Whitelock.

Addenda et Corrigenda to Vol. XVII
p. xxxv, l. 15 from bottom. For '132' read '123.'

p. 1, *s.n.* NOTTINGHAMSHIRE. Dr O. K. Schram informs us that the form *Snotingham* occurs in an account of the shires and hundreds of England in MS Jesus Coll. Oxford 29, which is dated c. 1275. This looks like a copy of an earlier document, but the copyist did not see fit to modernise this name as he did some of the others, so it may be that forms with S- existed in the 13th century.

p. 1, *s.n.* BACK DYKE. For '(Trent by Cotham)' read '(Devon by Cotham).'

p. 15, *s.n.* BRIDLESMITH GATE. Mr A. C. Wood draws attention to Roger de Flerdon 'bridelsmyth,' mentioned 1321–4 Pat.

p. 22, *s.n.* *Hallifax lane.* Mr L. Illingworth Butler informs us that this name is not lost, as there is a turning off Pilcher Gate which is called Halifax Place.

p. 149, *s.n.* DUNKIRK. Earlier occurrences of the name are found 1776, 1783 in the *Records of the Borough of Nottingham* vii, pp. 141, 195 (A.C.W.).

p. 173, *s.n.* HARTSWELL FM. The name in Tax refers to the property of the Abbot of Swineshead. This is *Herteswell in Kenalton* in LP xiv, part i, no. 1056 (2) and 1056 (8), and the reference should therefore be transferred to Hartwells Fm in Kinoulton, p. 237 (A.C.W.).

p. 179, *s.n.* CHECKERS. An earlier form is *the littell Chekers* 1540 *MinAcct* (A.C.W.).

VOL. XVIII

THE PLACE-NAMES OF MIDDLESEX

Reviews of Vol. XVIII
MLR 38 (1943), 44–5, Dorothy Whitelock.
YWES 23 (1942), 25–6, Dorothy Whitelock.
RES 21 (1945), 76–7, P. H. Reaney.
TLS 11 April 1942 [B.D.].
Speculum 17 (1942), 436–8, F. P. Magoun, Jr.
Economic History Review 13 (1942–3), 131.
JEGP 42 (1943), 271–5, Robert L. Ramsay.

Addenda et Corrigenda to Vol. XVIII
p. xxx. Delete the last two lines.

p. xxxi, l. 18 from bottom. This refers to PN Wa, not to PN Ess, and should be transferred accordingly.

p. 27, *s.n.* ISLEWORTH. Dr P. H. Reaney suggests that the forms with *Th-* are due to misreading of *ȝ*. *Th* not uncommonly appears as *Y* in medieval documents, and *Y* from *ȝ* may have been interpreted as *Th* by confusion with *Y* from *þ*.

p. 31, *s.n.* *Elthorne Hundred.* Dr P. H. Reaney suggests that this is a parallel to Althorne (PN Ess 208), and contains *ǣled*, the name meaning 'burnt thorn-bush.'

p. 42, *s.n.* YIEWSLEY. Dr P. H. Reaney suggests that the phonological development was (*at*) *Wewesley* > (*at*) *Ewsley* > *Yewsley*. The loss of *W-* can be compared with that in names in *wudu-*, and in Ockendon (PN Ess 124–5) and Uxbridge and Uxendon (PN Mx 48, 54).

p. 45, *s.n.* WAXLOW FM. Mr G. M. Bark has sent us the following references to a place called Bixley in this district: *Bexleye* 1293–4 *Ass*, *Bykley Field* 1514–15 *CourtR*, *Bixley Field* Hayes *EnclA*. It is probable that the 13th century form *Buxle* belongs to this name, the etymology being 'box wood.'

p. 54, *s.n.* WEALDSTONE. In a letter to the *Harrow Observer and Gazette*, 20 January 1949, Mr P. Davenport mentions two earlier references to the Weald Stone. In *Harrow Court Rolls* for 1507–8 "Richard Bukberd ought to cleanse his ditch lying between le Weld and le stone," and in 1522–3 "It is ordered that John Smith shall cleanse his ditch at the stone in Harrowe Lane."

p. 79, *s.n.* MITCHLEY MARSH. Add '*Minchley* 1636, 1640, 1667, 1719, *Mitchley Marsh* 1780, *Midgeley Ditch* 1812 *Place-Names of Walthamstow*, P. H. Reaney, p. 27.' Dr Reaney thinks these forms indicate confusion with *myncen*, perhaps because the nuns of Clerkenwell had property in the neighbourhood. The Marsh is still marked on the 6″ map of Essex.

p. 112, *s.n.* CHALK FM. Mr F. C. S. Gardner informs us that when his grandfather built his house on the outskirts of St John's Wood in 1841 the area now known as Chalk Fm was still known as *Chalcot's Farm*. Members of the *Chalcot* family were still living in the district 35 years ago.

p. 142, *s.n.* KEN WOOD. Add '*Canewood* 1530 *Court Rolls of the Rectory Manor, Walthamstow*, P. H. Reaney.' Dr Reaney suggests that the name is 'Canons' wood,' from the Canons of Aldgate. It is mentioned as belonging to the Prior of Holy Trinity, Aldgate, in the above reference.

p. 165, *s.n.* ST CLEMENT DANES. An earlier attempt than Stow's to account for the name is to be found in the *Vita et Passio Waldevi*, in a strange legend that makes Siward slay Earl Tostig on a bridge near Westminster, and claims that Tostig and his followers were buried "in territorio quodam prope Londonias; et in memoriam rei sic gestae constructa fuit ibi ecclesia quaedam, quae Ecclesia Dacorum appellata est usque in hodiernum diem." This is usually assumed to refer to St Clement Danes (D.W. in MLR 38).

p. 237. 'Ousterley (Du)' should be 'Austerley (Du).'

We are indebted to Mr C. R. Goodchild for the following notes:

p. 122, *s.n.* BROWNS WOOD. Part of the South Hornsey Ward of Stoke Newington Borough is still called Brownswood Division.

pp. 126–7. Add the following Islington street-names. 'CLOUDESLEY TERRACE AND SQUARE are named from Richard *Cloudesley*, who owned land here in the early 16th century (Tomlins 189). COLEBROOK TERRACE is named from John *Colebrook*, who was lord of the manor of Highbury in 1723 (Tomlins 124).'

p. 159, under STOKE NEWINGTON Borough add 'WOODBURY DOWN. Cf. *Wood Berry Down Meadow* 1734 RobinsonSN.' Under NOTE add 'DEFOE RD and HOWARD RD are named from Daniel *Defoe* and John *Howard* (RobinsonSN 96). EDE RD is named from Jonathan *Eade*, who bought the lease of the manor in 1783 (RobinsonSN 42). FLEETWOOD RD is the site of Fleetwood Ho, home of Cromwell's General Fleetwood.'

E. Ekwall (*Studia Neophilologica* 17 (1944), 25–34) has notes on Astlam, Chelsea, Weir Hall and Birchin Lane.

VOL. XIX

THE PLACE-NAMES OF CAMBRIDGESHIRE

Reviews of Vol. XIX

MLR 39 (1944), 65–7, S. Potter.
YWES 24 (1943), 22–4, Dorothy Whitelock.
History 29 (1944), 203, David Douglas.
Antiquity 18 (1944), 211–13, F. T. Wainwright.
TLS 21 August 1943 [B.D.].
NQ 185 (1943), 119–20.
Cambridge Review 20 Nov. 1943, A. J. Robertson.

Vols. XVIII and XIX

AntiqJ 24–5 (1944–5), 86–8.

Addenda et Corrigenda to Vol. XIX

p. liii, l. 4 from bottom. For '235' read '89.'

p. lv, l. 30. For '*Sparhauekesbeia*' read '*Sparhauekesheia*.'

p. 39, *s.n.* BARNWELL. For 'childrens' spring' read 'children's spring' (NQ 185).

p. 61. The Rev. F. C. Clare, F.S.A., informs us that the steeple of Steeple Morden church did not fall in 1703, but in 1625: this being the date given in the Depositions dated 1632, taken in connection with Bishop Matthew Wren's Visitation, and printed in *Documents Relating to Cambridgeshire Villages*, no. iv, W. M. Palmer and H. W. Saunders, C.U.P. 1926.

p. 88. CAIUS COLLEGE FARM. The record of a manor court held in 1774 shows that the earlier name was *Buristead* (StudNP xxiii, 113); cf. Burystead Fm in Sutton (PN C 241), etc.

p. 299. Delete '(n)' after ǣl and blāc.

p. 303. Delete '(n)' after hunig.

p. 304. Delete '(n)' after sceolh. (These errors were pointed out by S. Potter in MLR 39.)

p. 357, last paragraph. *Hen and chickens* is given in EDD (*s.v. hen* 2) as a dialect term for eleven kinds of plant.

p. 395. For 'Bestwall (Do), 146' read 'Bestwall (Do), 239.'

VOLS. XX AND XXI

THE PLACE-NAMES OF CUMBERLAND, PARTS I AND II

Reviews of Vols. XX and XXI (Cu)

TLS 1 September 1950.

The Cumberland News 30 September 1950.

The Whitehaven News 19 October 1950, T. Quayle.

MLR 46 (1951), 470–1, K. R. Brooks.

CW 50 (1951), 220–1.

EngSt 33 (1952), 67–71, O. Arngart.

Addenda et Corrigenda to Vols. XX and XXI

For '*v.* coninger' and '*v.* snabbi' read '*v.* cony-garth' and '*v.* snab.'

p. 20, *s.n.* LOSTRIGG BECK. For '*ric*' read '**ric*.'

pp. 32–7. For a much more extensive collection of modern forms of these lake-names see P. Thorsen, JEGP 30 (1931), 26–47.

p. 42, *s.n.* CARLISLE. PETRIANAE is Stanwix across the Eden, *v.* 512 *infra*.

p. 42, *s.n.* BOTCHERBY. Mr J. E. B. Gover points out that the personal name is to be found also in Botcheston in Ratby (Lei), *Bochardeston* 1309, 1312, Cl.

p. 53, *s.n.* NETHERBY. Col. Sir Edward Johnson-Ferguson has drawn our attention to a place called Middlebie in Dumfriesshire, marked on the 1″ map about 11 miles from Netherby, for which he has noted the forms *Middeby* 1291 Ragman Roll, *Mydilby* 1349 Historical MSS, Queensberry Papers. The church has all the appearance of being on the site of an old camp; it is very near the line of the Roman road which runs over the shoulder of Birrenswark and up Annandale. Birrenswark was a celebrated Roman camp and Middlebie is on a straight line between Netherby and Birrenswark. This is very probably Hutchinson's camp called Middleby.

pp. 70–1, *s.n.* CALEES. Mr Gover compares The Callis, a street-name in Ashby de la Zouch (Lei), *Caleys* 1445 Hastings MSS (HMC), *Callis* 1622 Wills, presumably from the French place-name Calais.

p. 71, *s.n.* LANERCOST, p. 72, *s.n. Lanrekaythin*, p. 115, *s.n.* LANERTON. For 'grove' read 'glade.'

p. 95, *s.n.* CARGO. Mr Gover points out that the Cornish form is *carrec*, not *carreg*.

p. 109, *s.n.* STANWIX. For 'CONGAVATA' read 'PETRIANAE.' See p. 512 *infra*.

p. 120, *s.n.* WIGGONBY. For '(Chrest 172)' read '(Chrest 174).'

p. 125, *s.n.* FINGLAND. Mr J. E. B. Gover informs us that Fingland in Tweedsmuir, Peebles, is *Fynglen* in 1371 (*Origines parochiales Scotiae*).

p. 132, last line. For 'Devoke Water (La)' read 'Devoke Water (33).'

p. 134, *s.n.* LAKEWOLF. Mr J. E. B. Gover has found an apparent parallel to this in the name *Lecbernard* (1203, *Origines parochiales Scotiae*, ed. Cosmo Innes, Bannatyne Cl. 1850–5). The name occurs in the boundaries of Romanno in Newlands parish, Peeblesshire, and is identified by James Buchan (*History of Peeblesshire*) with Leadburn, just over the county boundary in Midlothian.

p. 202, *s.n.* CARAVERICK. With the second element Mr Gover compares Breton *havrek* 'fallowland' and Treharrock in St Kew (Co), *Trehaverek* 1284 MinAcct.

p. 204, *s.n.* TARN WADLING. Mr Gover compares Trewidland in Liskeard (Co), *Trewythelan* 1298 MinAcct.

p. 227, *s.n.* NEWTON REIGNY. Mr Gover compares Ashreigny (PN D 355).

p. 243, *s.n.* CROSS FELL. Mr J. E. B. Gover has noted the following parallel to the old name *Fendesfell*. In a description of Tweeddale in *Macfarlane's Geographical Collections* iii, p. 152 (Scottish History Soc. 53) it is stated: "Upon the head of this fertile Water above Glenkirk is a mountain called *Fiendsfell*...." A study of a map of this district suggests that Fiendsfell may have been the old name of Culter Fell on the Peebles-Lanarkshire border.

p. 246, *s.n.* THISTLEWOOD. Add '*Thistlewood* 1704 CW 50.'

p. 253, *s.n.* SADDLEBACK OR BLENCATHRA. Add '*Saddle-Back or Blenk-Arthur* 1704 CW 50.'

p. 254, *s.n.* WATERMILLOCK. Mr Gover compares Millock in Poundstock (Co), *Mellok* 1284 Ass.

p. 255, *s.n.* MAIDENCASTLE. With the second element of *Carthanack* Mr Gover compares Tredannick in Egloshayle (Co), *Trethanek* 1360 Ct. The p.n. *Danoc* occurs in Liber Landavensis.

pp. 259–60, *s.n.* BAGGROW. Mr F. Williamson informs us that East Street, Derby, was formerly *Baggelone* 13th, 1327–8, *Bagelone* 1461, *Baglone* 1469: in this instance he thinks the name meant 'lane shaped like a bag,' i.e. closed at one end, a cul-de-sac. There was also a *Bagge Lone* in Congleton (1264, Db. Arch. and Nat. Hist. Soc. Journal 1942).

p. 267, *s.n.* REDMAIN. Mr Gover points out that this name is to be recognised in the earlier forms for Polridmouth in Fowey (Co).

p. 276, *s.n.* CALDBECK FELLS. Add '*Caldbeck-Fells* 1704 CW 50.'

p. 292, *s.n.* RABY. For (v)rá read rá.

p. 297. ST ROCHE'S CHAPEL. Since the footnote was written 'Le problème de Saint Roch' has been admirably elucidated by A. Fliche in AB 68 (1950), 343–61. Born, probably in Montpellier, about 1350, the Saint set out on pilgrimage to Rome and, stopping at Acquapendente and Cesena where the plague was at its height, effected many miraculous cures. After being in Rome from c. 1368 to c. 1371, then in Rimini, Novara and Piacenza (where he himself survived an attack of the plague), he was on his way home when he was seized as a spy at Angleria, where he died after five years (c. 1374–9) in prison. A century later his body was taken to Venice, where most English visitors are familiar with the Scuola di San Rocco. He was canonised by the Avignon pope Benedict XIII (elected 1394 and several times deposed before his death in 1422) and his cult, quite understandably, spread over Western Europe before the Reformation. It was celebrated on 16 August. Add to the dedications chantries in the churches of Pontefract and Sherburn-in-Elmet WRY (*Surtees Soc.* 92, 226, 275, 401).

p. 303, *s.n.* MONK HALL. Add 'The site is now occupied by the Keswick Hospital.'

p. 306, *s.n.* MARYPORT. The Roman fort is of course that at Ellenborough (284–6).

p. 322, *s.n.* ORMATHWAITE. *v.* p. 486 *infra*.

p. 339, *s.n.* FARMERY. Delete the sentence beginning 'The earliest example.'

p. 347, *s.n.* MOPUS. Mr J. E. B. Gover informs us that Malpas in Cornwall is *Molpus* or *Mopus* in 1651, earlier *Malpasse* in 1613. (Forms from Henderson MSS at Truro.)

p. 347, *s.n.* SEATON HALL. For '*lēce*' read '*lece*.'

p. 389, *s.n.* RYSEBRIGGE, Miss M. C. Fair tells us that this bridge was mentioned in a schedule of road repairs of 1847, as *Ryse Brigg*. It is now a bridge of flat large stone slabs over a stream running between Chriscliffe and Peel Place.

p. 393, under field-names, Miss M. C. Fair tells us that the present Church Lane was known in 1840 as *Ele Beck Lane*.

p. 394, *s.n.* GREASON COTTAGE. Miss M. C. Fair informs us that she has seen a 'great grey stone' here: it was blown up by a farmer c. 1944–5.

p. 404, *s.n.* PUGHOUSE WOOD. For 'heating of clay' read 'beating of clay.'

p. 408, *s.n.* HOBCARTON. Mr J. E. B. Gover suggests that an identical name may be Hopecarton in Peeblesshire, which is *Hopecarthan* c. 1240, *Hopcarthane* 1291 (forms from *Origines parochiales Scotiae*, ed. Cosmo Innes, 1850–5), the first element of which is probably OE *hop*.

p. 424, *s.n.* BARNSCAR. Miss M. C. Fair informs us that *Remains of the City of Barnsea* refers to a fiction invented by Aaron Marshall, curate of Eskdale, who wished it on Hutchinson as a Danish city and described streets etc., which were pure imagination. There are Bronze Age cairns and foundations and a few Bronze Age huts there.

p. 453, *s.n.* HARRAS. For 'ON' read 'OE.'

CUMBERLAND

THE ELEMENTS, APART FROM PERSONAL NAMES, FOUND IN CUMBERLAND PLACE-NAMES

Under each element the examples are arranged in three categories, (*a*) uncompounded elements and examples in which the first element is a significant word or another place-name, not a personal name, (*b*) those in which the first element, or, in the case of inversion compounds, the second element, is a personal name, (*c*) those in which the character of the first element is uncertain. Inversion compounds in which the second element is not a personal name have been placed under (*a*). Where no statement is made it may be assumed that the examples belong to type (*a*). Names for which no forms earlier than 1500 have been found are only included if they are of special interest.

á, ON, 'river.' Aira Beck, Ameshaugh, Borrowdale (?), Greta, Ive, Keekle (?), Liza, Roe Beck. The forms for Aira Beck, Liza and Roe Beck show that these names contain an early form of the word with the original voiceless spirant preserved.

āc, OE, 'oak.' Oakshaw. Also in field-names and minor names for which there are only late forms.

æcer, OE, 'cultivated piece of land.' Uzzicar, Weddicar. This word and the corresponding ON **akr** occur in field-names.

ǣdre, OE, 'artery, vein' also 'watercourse.' *Edderlanghals* (?), Edderside. *Edderlanghals* may contain the OE adjective which gives the adverb *ǣdre*, 'quickly.'

ǣl, OE, 'eel.' *Eelchist*, Eel Beck, Eel Sike.

ælf, OE, 'elf, fairy,' probably occurs in Elf Hall and Elva Hill, and is found in four field-names meaning 'elf hill' (*Elnehull* 1355, *Elvehull* 1359 Carlisle, *Elfhow* 1488 et seq. Hutton-in-the-Forest, *Elvinhowe* 1577 Gosforth and *Elfe Hill* 1578 Aspatria).

æppel, OE, 'apple.' Applethwaite ('Apple tree' þveit occurs about six times as a field-name).

æppeltūn, OE, 'orchard.' Appleton Hall.

æsc, OE, 'ash.' Ash, Ashy Cleugh, Ashycroft.

æspe, OE, 'aspen.' Isthmus (?). Occasionally in field-names, cf. *the Asphill* 1603 in Cumrew.

afnám, a word of Scandinavian origin, identical in meaning with **intak** *infra*, occurs in two medieval field-names, *Ofnames* (c. 1290 in Wetheral) and *Avena'croftes* (c. 1270 in Stainburn).

(e)ald, OE, 'old.' Albyfield, Aldby (2), Aldoth, Aughertree.

allan, a Cumberland dialect word for 'a bit of land nearly surrounded by water: an island,' possibly connected with Gaelic *eilean*, occurs frequently in field-names. Cf. *the Allands* (1582 in Above Derwent) and Allans, Allons (modern in Millom and Crosby-on-Eden).

alor, OE, 'alder.' Aldersceugh, Seatoller (?). Also in field-names.

***anger**, OE, 'grassland.' Angerton (2). Occurs in field-names.

ar, British preposition, 'on.' *Dollerline*, Newton Arlosh (?).

(e)arn, OE, 'eagle.' Arlecdon.

askr, ON, 'ash.' (*b*) Aspatria.

austr, ON, 'east.' Easthwaite.

averys, ME from OFr, 'eatage of arable land after harvest.' Ambrose Holme.

bæcestre, OE, 'baker.' Baxter's Row.

bagge, ME, 'bag.' Baggara, Baggra Yeat, Baggrow.

baillie, ME from OFr, 'district under the jurisdiction of a bailiff.' Bailey, Baileyhead.

***bakstǎn**, ME, 'bakestone, a flat stone on which cakes are baked in the oven.' Baxton Gill, Baystone Bank Fm, Beckstones, Beckstones Gill, Beckstone Gate. The word occurs several times in field-names.

bali, ON, 'gentle slope.' Bayles (?).

bank(e), ME, 'bank.' Bank, Banks, Bankend (2), Bank Hall, Blackbank Cottage, Brownbank, Burbank Ho, Ellen Bank, Haile Bank, Hall Bank (2), *Hallebanke*, High Bankhill, Hullerbank, Kellbank, Kirkbank, Roebanks, Rowantree Bank, Rubby Banks, Thornbank, Whinbank, Wodow Bank, Yew Bank. Fairly frequent in field-names.

baron, ME from OFr, 'manorial lord.' Baronwood.

barres, barwis, ME from OFr *barras*, 'barrier.' Barras (3), Barrass Gate. Occasionally in field-names.

barroc, a hill-name of British origin, derived from an OCeltic *barro-, 'top, crest.' Barrock.

batayle, ME from OFr, in the sense 'judicial duel.' Battail Holme.

bating, present participle of a shortened form of the verb *debate*. Batenbush. Debateable Land was earlier *the Batable Lande*.

bēam, OE, 'tree.' Kirkbampton.

bēan, OE, 'bean.' Benwray. Occasionally in field-names. ON **baun**, 'bean,' may be the first element of Bowten Beck.

beinn, ON, 'straight.' Bannest Hill (?).

beinviðr, ON, 'holly.' Bennethead.

bekkr, ON, 'stream.' (*a*) Beckermet, *Beksneuell*, Aira Beck, *Aisthwaite bek*, Birker Beck, Birkett Beck, Bitter Beck, Black Beck (2), Blencarn Beck, Bowten Beck, Briggle Beck, Bustabeck, Caldbeck, Cald Beck, Crookley Beck, Crossdale Beck, Cumrew Beck, Cumwhitton Beck, Dacre Beck, Dry Beck, Dub Beck, Eller Beck (3), Ellerbeck, Farlam Beck, *Frithebec*, Grise Beck, *Holebech*, Hole Beck, *Holegatebeck*, How Beck, Kirk Beck, Langrigg Beck, Linbeck, Linbeck Gill, Line Beck, Logan Beck, Longstrath Beck, Mere Beck (2), Merebeck Gill, Millbeck (2), Mosedale Beck, Nor Beck, Over Beck, Routenbeck, Scalebeck Gill, Silver Beck, Skill Beck, Skirting Beck, Sleet Beck, Tarn Beck, Thornthwaite Beck, Troutbeck, Trout Beck (3), Whit Beck (2), Whitbeck, Wythop Beck; (*b*) *bek Troyte*, Snary Beck; (*c*) Capplebeck. Occurs *passim* in field-names, and minor names for which the forms are late.

beonet, OE, 'bent-grass.' The modern name Bent(s) is common among field and minor names.

be(o)rg, OE, 'hill.' (*a*) Brackenbarrow, Brackenbrough Tower, Buck Barrow (2), Crossbarrow, Gallowbarrow, Gallowberry, Hayborough, Longburgh, Thornbarrow (2), Whinbarrow, Whitbarrow Hall, Yewbarrow. **berg**, ON, 'hill.' (*a*) *Berh*, Berrier, Caber, Harberry Beck, *Houtbergh*, Kelbarrow, Long Barrow, *Scoggarbar*; (*b*) Legburthwaite; (*c*) Gowbarrow, Rainsbarrow Wood. The two elements appear in field-names, and Barf is fairly frequent as a minor name for which only late forms are available. In some names in the above lists it is impossible to be certain whether the element was originally OE or ON.

bield, northern dialect, 'a place of shelter,' occurs occasionally in field and minor names, generally preceded by an animal name. Cf. Fox Bield in Birker.

bi(e)rce, OE, 'birch.' Birkett Beck, Birkett Mire, Brisco. The adjective *bi(e)rcen* is the first element of *Byrkensydvanell*, a lost street-name in Carlisle.

(wudu)binde, OE, 'woodbine.' Binthwaite Plantation.

birki, ON, 'birch.' Birchclose, Birchtimber Hill, Birker, Birkmere Wood, Birkmire, Birkrigg. Often difficult to distinguish from OE bi(e)rce *supra*.

bischop, ME, 'bishop.' Bishop's Row, Bustabeck.

bitts. The meaning is uncertain, but *Bitts* or *The Bitts* occurs five times as a field-name, and *Ackbitts, oak bitts, Busy bitt, Shirraforth Bitt, Mean bit* have also been noted. The forms are 16th century or later.

blá(r), ON, 'dark.' Black Beck, Blagill, Blea Beck, Bleagate, Bleatarn, Blea Tarn, Bleawath, Botlands Blawith. The river-name Bleng represents an ON blæingr, a derivative of blá(r).

blabery, ME, 'blaeberry.' *Blaburthwaite*.

blāc, OE, 'pale,' i.e. 'foaming.' Black Burn.

blæc, OE, 'black.' Black Beck (2), Black Comb (2), Black Fell, Blackford, Blackhall, Black Lyne, Black Pots, Black Sike.

blæcberie, OE, 'blackberry.' Bleaberry Gill.

*blæcþorn, OE, 'blackthorn.' Blitterlees (?).

blaen, Welsh, 'top.' A British word corresponding to this is the first element of Blencarn, Blencathra, Blencogo, Blencow (2), Blennerhasset, Blindcrake.

bleikr, ON, 'pale.' Black Burn, Blaithwaite.

blesi, ON, 'white spot.' Blaze Bridge (?), Blaze Fell.

blind, OE, 'blind'; applied to springs or streams in the sense 'hidden by vegetation.' Blind Keld, Blind Tarn (2).

boga, OE, 'bow, arch.' Bow, Bowbank, Bowness (?), Bowscale (2), Bowthorn. Bowness may contain the corresponding ON **bogi**.

borg, ON, 'fortress.' Borrowdale.

bōþ, ODan, 'booth, temporary shelter.' (*a*) Boat How; (*c*) Armboth.

búð, ON, identical in meaning. (*a*) Bewcastle, Bowderdale, Burthwaite Bridge, Waberthwaite; (*b*) Brotherilkeld.

*bōðl, **bōtl**, OE, 'dwelling, house, palace.' (*a*) Bootle, Bothel; (*c*) Blindbothel. Bootle is from **bōtl**.

*bōðltūn, OE, compound of ***bōðl** and **tūn**, possibly used of the 'village proper' in contrast to the surrounding outlying land. Bolton Hall, Boltons.

botm, OE, **botn**, ON, 'valley.' Wythburn.

bouȝt, ME, 'bend, turn.' Boot.

brād, OE, 'broad.' Bradley, Broadfield, Broad Field, Broadwath. Fairly common in field-names.

bræc, OE, 'land newly taken into cultivation,' occurs only in three field-names, *Brakhalethwayt* (1345 in Caldbeck), *Breeches* (1722 in Kirkandrews upon Eden) and Breeches Peice (modern in Millom). It is a very common field-name element in some counties.

brǣd, OE, 'breadth, width,' used in place-names of a broad strip of land, occurs once in the field-name *Stanebrede* (c. 1220 Whitbeck) and possibly in the compound *garbrade*, for which *v. infra*.

braken, ME, 'bracken.' Brackenbarrow, Brackenbrough Tower, Bracken Hill (2), Brackenhill Tower, Bracken How, Brackenrigg, Brackenriggs, Brackenthwaite (4), Brecon Hill. The northern dialect form of the word is represented by Brecon Hill, and there are spellings with -*e*- in the 16th century or later for a number of these names.

brame, ME, 'briar, bramble.' Bramery, Brampton, Branthwaite (?), Branthwaite.

brant, OE, 'steep.' Bransty.

breiðr, ON, 'broad.' Brae Fell, Braithmoor, Braithwaite (2), Braystones, Brayton. Also in field-names.

brend, ME, 'burnt.' Brundholme (?), Brunt Knott, Burnthwaite. Fairly frequent in field-names, where there are two 'burnt chapels' (Aikton and Penrith), two 'burnt shielings' (Arthuret and Castle Carrock), a 'burnt þveit' (Dalston) and a 'burnt tree stump' (Birker), for which the forms are medieval, and a number of similar modern names.

brere, ME, 'briar.' Bruthwaite Forest.

Breta, ON, 'of the Britons.' Birkby (2), Briscoe.

brinke, brenke, ME, 'edge.' *Burntippet* (?).

brōc, OE, 'brook.' Broughton.

brocc-hol, OE, 'badger set.' Brocklebank, Brocklewath (?). Occurs several times in field-names.

brōm, OE, 'broom.' *Brangull*, Broomfield, Brownhow Hill.

brot, OE and ON, 'fragment.' Broats Plantation, Brotto (?). Occurs several times in field-names.

brūn, OE, 'brown.' Bromfield (?), Brownbank, Brown Dodd, Brownrigg (4), Brunshaw Moss. Brownrigg may contain the corresponding ON **brúnn**.

bruni, ON, 'place cleared by burning.' Brunstock, *Brunskaith*.

brycg, OE, 'bridge.' (*a*) Bridge End, Bridgewood Foot, Brigham (2), Blennerhasset Bridge, Caldew Bridge, Chalkbridge, Derwent Bridge, Duddon Bridge, Eden Bridges, Egremont Bridge, Ellen Bridge, Gatesgill Bridge, Gill Bridge, Haltcliff Bridge, Kingbridge, Long Bridge, Ouse Bridge, Petteril Bridge, *la Quarelbryg*, *Rysebrigge*, Sebergham Bridge, Stockbridge, Warwick Bridge, Waverbridge; (*b*) *Briggethorfin*. Common in field and minor names, where there are three 'foul bridges,' several more 'stock bridges' and more than one 'stone bridge.'

bryggja, ON, 'jetty, quay.' Bridge Petton (?), Brig Stones.

bryn, British, 'hill.' Knorren Beck (?).

bú, ON, 'homestead.' (*b*) Bewaldeth.

buarth, Welsh, 'a farmyard, fold.' A British word corresponding to this is the first element of Burtholme Beck.

bucc, OE, 'buck.' Buck Barrow. The corresponding ON **bukkr** occurs in a field-name in Whitbeck.

burghan, ME, 'burial mound,' apparently cognate with OE **byrgen**. Baron Side, Borrowscale (2), Burns Rigg, Sewborwens. Very frequent in field-names from the 13th century onwards, and found in a number of minor names for which only late forms are available.

burh, OE, 'fortified place, town, manor house.' Burgh by Sands, Burbank Ho, Burrowgate, Ellenborough, Mawbray, Nentsberry, *Powburgh*, Skinburness, Turnberry Ho.

burhstede, OE, 'site of a burh.' Boustead Hill.

burna, OE, 'stream.' Burnfoot, Burnhope Seat, Banks Burn, Black Burn, Crook Burn (2), Crookburn, Dryburn, Gilderdale Burn, Green's Burn, Hartley Burn, How Burn, Lot Burn, *Mereburn*, Rae Burn, Roachburn, Stainburn. Occurs also in field-names, and minor names for which the forms are very late.

burtree, northern dialect word meaning 'elder tree,' first recorded c. 1450, occurs in the field-names of Caldbeck, Dean, Middlesceugh, Penrith and Skelton. The forms date from the 13th century onwards.

buskr, ON, 'bush,' occurs occasionally in field-names (cf. *Elrebusche*, c. 1245 in Farlam) and is probably the second element of Birch Bush and Birk Bush in Askerton.

butere, OE, 'butter,' used in place-names to describe rich pasturage. Buttermere. Occasionally in field-names, *v. infra* Fan.

butte, ME, used of strips of ground abutting on a boundary, often at right angles to other ridges in the field. This word is very common in field and minor names, often occurring in the plural. Cf. *Trendilbut* (a. 1240 in Burgh by Sands) and *Moonebutts* (1633 in Blencogo), both presumably named from their shape, and the former containing OE *trendel*, 'circle.'

bwch, Welsh, 'buck.' A corresponding British word may be the second element of Drumburgh.

bwrdd, Welsh, 'table.' A British word corresponding to this is the first element of (*b*) Birdoswald.

bȳ, late OE from ON *bȳr*, *bœr*, Swed, Dan *by*, 'village, hamlet.' (*a*) Albyfield, Aldby (2), Allerby, Birkby (2), Crosby-on-Eden, Crosscanonby, Flimby, Hunsonby, Ireby, *Kirkeby Beycok*, *Kirkeby Crossan*, *Kirkeby Johannis*, Langwathby, Lazonby, Netherby, Newby (2), Overby, Parsonby, Raby, Scaleby, Scotby, Southernby, Castle Sowerby, Sowerby Wood, Walby; (*b*) Aglionby, *Aldeneby*, Allonby, Alstonby, Arkleby, Arnaby, Boothby, Botcherby, Corby, Dolphenby, Dovenby, Easby, Farmanby, Ellonby, Etterby, Gamblesby, Gamelsby, Glassonby, Gutterby (2), Harraby, Hornsby, *Isaacby*, Johnby, Laconby, Lamonby, Maughonby, Melmerby, Moresby, Motherby, *Ormesby*, Oughterby, Ousby, Ponsonby, Rickerby, Robberby, Skitby, Soulby, Tarraby, Thursby, Upmanby, Upperby, Wiggonby; (*c*) Swabies, *Thirneby*, Thornby, *Ureby Field*, Wormanby. There is another *Aldeby* in the field-names of Blindcrake.

bygg, ON, 'barley.' Biglands, Bigrigg. Occurs also in field-names.

bygging, ME of Norse origin, 'building.' (*a*) Newbiggin (4); (*b*) *Nelesbigginge*.

bȳre, OE, 'shed, hovel.' Byerstead, Abbey Cowper, Lowbyer. *Birestede* occurs also as a field-name in Crosscanonby.

cack, ME, 'to void excrement.' Catlowdy.

caer, Welsh, 'fortified place.' A British word corresponding to this is the first element of Caermote, *Caraverick*, Cardew, Cardunneth Pike, Cardunnock, Carlisle, Carthanack, Carwinley. An adjectival form corresponding to Welsh *caerog*, 'fortified,' occurs in Castle Carrock.

cærse, OE, 'cress.' *Carswelhowe*, Kershope (?).

cæster, OE (Anglian), 'city or walled town, ancient fort.' (*a*) Cast Rigg (?), Bewcastle, Papcastle; (*b*) Muncaster, *Palme Castell*.

*caino-, suggested by Ekwall (RN 178–9) as the Celtic base from which the river-name Glencoyne has developed.

*caiton, British, 'wood.' (*a*) Culgaith; (*c*) Clesketts.

c(e)ald, OE, 'cold.' Caldecotes, Caldew. Occasionally in field-names.

caled, Welsh, 'rapid.' A British word corresponding to this is found in Calder.

c(e)alf, OE, 'calf.' Calfgarth Plantation, Calfhow Pike, Calthwaite, Calva Hall, Calvo. In the compound with **haugr**, several times repeated, the word *calf* may be used in the same way as when it denotes a small island situated near a larger one. This is suggested by Ekwall (PN La 194) as the explanation of the name Caw in La.

camb, OE, 'comb, ridge.' The Combs, Coombs Clint, Black Comb (2), Dry Comb.

*cambāco-, British, 'crooked.' Cam Beck, Cammock Beck.

can, Welsh, 'white.' A British word corresponding to this may be the second element of Talkin.

canon, ME from OFr, 'canon.' Crosscanonby.

capel, ME ultimately from Latin *caballus*, 'nag,' occurs about half-a-dozen times in field and minor names. Cf. *Capeltrebek* (c. 1203 in Mosser), *Caplecragge* (1587 in Eskdale) and Capell Crag (on the map in Borrowdale), *the caple croft* (1589 in Askerton), *Caplefield* (1633 in Blencogo).

carn, Welsh, 'a heap of stones.' A British word corresponding to this occurs in (*a*) Cairn Beck, Blencarn; (*b*) Carnetley.

carrecc, British, 'rock.' Cargo, Carrock Fell.

castel, OE from Latin, 'castle, fort.' (*a*) Castlerigg, Castle Slack, Castle Sowerby, Castlesteads (2), Castle St, Bewcastle (replacing **cæster**), Carlisle Castle, Egremont Castle, Greystoke Castle, High Head Castle, Lazencastle, Maidencastle, Wolsty Castle; (*b*) Castle Hewin. Also in field-names. Castle Carrock contains an identical British word, a borrowing from Latin *castellum*.

cat, ME and Gaelic, 'wild cat.' Catgill Hall, Cathow, *Catlogan*.

cateir, OWelsh, 'chair,' occasionally used of a mountain. The corresponding British word occurs in Catterlen, *Caterlaising*.

ceann, Gaelic, 'head.' Cannerheugh (?), King Harry, Kinkry Hill (?), Kinmont, Kinniside (?), Torkin (?).

c(ī)ese, OE, 'cheese.' Keswick.

chapele, ME from OFr, 'chapel.' Chapel Burn (2), Chapelburn, Chapel Field. Also in field-names and minor names for which the forms are very late.

cil, OWelsh, 'retreat.' The corresponding British word occurs in Culgaith, Gilcrux.

clas, Welsh, 'glebe.' A corresponding British word may be the first element of Clesketts.

clif, OE, 'cliff, slope, bank of a river.' Cliff, Clifton.

clife, cliþe, OE, 'burdock.' Cleahall (?).

clōh, OE, 'clough, ravine': only found as a place-name element in the north. Cloffocks, Closegill, Clowsgill Holme, Haltcliff Hall. *cleugh* is fairly common in minor names for which there are only 16th century or later forms, and *cleugh, clough, clugh* are common in field-names.

close, ME, 'enclosure.' Birchclose. Common in field-names.

cnæpp, OE, 'summit of a hill, short sharp ascent,' occurs in field and minor names. It is probably the second element of Grassnop in Hutton-in-the-Forest and the first element of Knapethorn in Allhallows.

cnau, British, 'nuts.' Knorren Beck (?).

cnocc, OIrish, 'hillock, spike.' (*a*) *Cnokdentwald*; (*b*) Knockupworth.

cnoll, OE, 'knoll, summit.' Knowe, Rob's Knowe, Stoneknow. *know(e)* is very common in field and minor names. **cnylle*, a mutated derivative, is the probable source of Knells.

cocksho(o)t, ME, 'glade in a wood through which woodcocks might dart or "shoot," so as to be caught by nets stretched across the opening.' *Wodekokshotes*. Also occurs about eight times in field and minor names for which no early forms are available.

cog, Welsh, 'cuckoo.' A corresponding British word may occur in Blencogo.

cokelayk, ME. The term is recorded only in EDD, where it is defined as 'a spot frequented by grouse.' The second element is ON **leikr**, 'play.' Lady Henley suggests that the reference is to the mating dance of the grouse, which is a very striking spectacle. There are forms earlier than 1650 for *Cocklayc*, Cocklakes, Cocklet Rigg, Cockleygill, Cockley Moss, and *le Cokelayk'* (1279) in Millom fields, the earliest form being for *Cocklayc* in 1189. The term also occurs in six field and minor names for which there are only modern forms. The synonymous term *cockplaie* occurs as a field-name in Kirkandrews (1603).

col, OE, 'charcoal.' Colmire Sough.

cony-garth, 'rabbit-warren,' a corruption of ME *conyng-erthe*, *conig-erthe*, 'cony earth,' occurs four times as Cunning Garth and once as Coneygarth in field and minor names. There are no forms earlier than the 16th century.

copp, OE, 'top, summit,' occurs once in Coneygarth Cop. The derivative **coppede**, which can mean either 'having the top cut off, pollarded' or 'rising to a peak,' occurs twice, with the former sense, in Copt Hill and Cop Thorn, the last being the name of a field in Lamplugh.

***corn**, ***cron**, OE, a side-form of **cran**, 'heron.' Corney.

corr, MIr, 'point, peak.' Corkickle (?).

cot(e), OE, 'cottage.' Coat Hill, Coathill, Cotehill, Aughertree, Caldecotes, East Cote, Raby Cote, Saltcoats, Salt Cotes, Seacote, Ulcat Row, Ulcoats.

cove, ME, here meaning 'recess.' Lingcove Beck. Occurs occasionally in minor names for which only late forms are available.

crag, ME, 'rock.' Crag, Craglands Sike, Black Crag, Dropping Crag, Gowder Crag, Rough Crag. Occurs also in field-names.

craicc, MIr, 'rock, cliff.' (*b*) Greysouthen.

creag, Gaelic, 'rock.' Kinkry Hill (?).

creic, OWelsh, 'rock.' A corresponding British word occurs in Crakeplace Hall, Greystoke (?), Blindcrake.

crew, Modern English (ME ***crue*?**), 'pen, cote.' Crew, Crewgarth. Crugarth occurs as a field-name in Cleator.

croesog, Welsh, 'having a cross.' A British word corresponding to this might be the second element of Tercrosset.

croft, OE, 'small enclosure.' (*a*) The Croft, Croft Fm, *Croftbathoc*, Croftend (3), Crofthouse, Crofton, Priestcroft, Ruckcroft, Silecroft, Whitecroft Bridge; (*b*) Croftmorris. Very common in field-names.

croked, ME, 'crooked.' Crook Burn (2), Crookburn, Crookdake.

cros, late OE (a Norse loan-word), 'cross.' (*a*) Crossbarrow, Crossfield, Crossgill, Crosslands, *Grith Cross*; (*b*) Mabil Cross. Also in field-names.

***croucā**, British, 'hill, mound.' Gilcrux, Cumcrook.

***crumbāco-**, British, 'crooked.' Crummock Beck, Crummock Water.

cū, OE, 'cow,' occurs occasionally in field and minor names. Cf. Cowlaw in Westward.

***cucrā**, British, 'crooked.' Cocker.

culdir, Welsh, 'narrow piece of land, isthmus.' A corresponding British word occurs in Coulderton, Holm Cultram.

cumbā, British, 'valley.' (*a*) Cumcatch, Cumcrook, Cumrenton, Cumrew, Cumwhitton; (*b*) *Couwhencatte*, Cumdivock, Cumwhinton.

*Cumbras, OE from Welsh *Cymry*, 'the Welsh.' Cumberland, Cummersdale.

currock, currick, a northern dialect word meaning 'cairn' or 'hill,' occurs some six times in field and minor names.

cyln, OE, 'kiln.' Kilnbank, Kiln Hill.

cyning, OE, 'king.' Kingbridge, Kingmoor, Kingside Hill.

dæl, OE, 'valley.' (*a*) Bewcastle Dale, Cummersdale, Eskdale Ward, Hawksdale, Liddel Water, Liddesdale, Sandale, Tindale, Woundell Beck; (*b*) Laversdale; (*c*) Priorsdale. **dalr**, ON, 'valley.' (*a*) Dale, Dalegarth, Allerdale, Borrowdale, Bowderdale, Crossdale, Crossdale Beck, Ennerdale, Eskdale, Geltsdale, Gilderdale Forest, Greendale, Keskadale, Little Dale, Matterdale, Miterdale, Moasdale, Mosedale, Mosedale Beck, Mungrisdale, Naddle, Rannerdale, High Scawdel, Stockdale, Uldale Fm, Wasdale; (*b*) Dalemain, Coledale; (*c*) Grinsdale, Uldale. It is not always possible to state with certainty whether the element is **dæl** or **dalr**: both occur also in field-names.

*dakru, British, 'tear.' Dacre.

dāl, OE, 'share in common land.' Longdales. Occurs once in a field-name (*le Howe Laund dole*, 1605 in Staffield).

dash, NED sb[4], 'the violent throwing or breaking of water upon or against anything,' is used of a waterfall in Dash and Whitewater Dash.

day-work, 'the amount of land that could be worked in a day,' is common in field and minor names in the forms Darg(u)e, Dark, Dack, Darrock, Dork, Day(s) Work. The forms are 16th century or later.

denu, OE, 'valley.' (*a*) Dean, Denton, Arlecdon; (*b*) Duddon (?).

dēor, OE, 'deer.' Dearham, Driggith Beck.

*derwā, British, 'oak.' Derwent.

Des. Descriptive terms which occur in the field and minor names of the county include:

    lot, denoting a piece of land assigned by lot, and *share*, 'a portion of land assigned to a particular holder' (NED). The former is rare compared to its use in other counties; it has been noted in Alston, Little Clifton, and Staffield. The latter occurs four times, cf. Little Shares in Bromfield and Small Shares in Great Salkeld.

    shank, either used in the northern dialect sense 'the projecting point of a hill, the narrow ridge which joins it to the plain' (NED), or simply meaning 'a narrow hill or strip of ground' occurs in Bewcastle, Kingwater, Kirkoswald, Scaleby, Solport and Stapleton.

Straits (modern in Alston) and *Strait Field* (c. 1840 in Millom) presumably describe a long, narrow strip of land.

sour, used of cold, wet land is frequent.

swath, ME, 'mark left by the scythe of the mower, measure of grass land,' occurs in Blencogo, Lorton and Great Salkeld.

There is one occurrence of each of the following terms: *grubbing* (17th century in Hesket, recorded also PN Sr 369, probably denoting land which has been grubbed up), *rainbow* (1809 in Dean, probably referring to land which is ploughed rainbow, i.e. parallel to the sides of a curving field), *roundabout* (modern in Whitbeck, this usually refers to a field with a clump of trees in the middle or surrounded by a wood).

dial. This element has been noted in several counties, *v.* PN Sx 188, PN Sr 368, PN Wa 155, PN Mx 205. The forms are 16th century or later, and no explanation has been suggested. In Cumberland the element occurs in Blue-dial and Red Dial, and in Dial Hill, found four times as a field-name. In *Notes and Queries* 185 (1943), 266–7, W. W. Gill made an interesting suggestion about such names, comparing the passage in *3 Henry VI*, II, v, 21–5:

> "O God! methinks it were a happy life
> To be no better than a homely swain;
> To sit upon a hill, as I do now,
> To carve out dials, quaintly, point by point,
> Thereby to see the minutes how they run...."

The dials in question are sun-dials, and Mr Gill quotes other references to shepherds carving these out of turf.

dīc, OE, 'ditch, dike.' Dykesfield, Hollowdyke Fm, Scots' Dike. **díki**, ON, 'ditch, dike.' Crindledike, Crindledyke. Also in field-names.

dind, OIr, 'hill.' Dent, *Cnokdentwald*.

docce, OE, 'dock, sorrel.' Dockray (3), Dock Tarn.

dod, ME (not recorded except in place-names until the 19th century), 'a rounded hill.' The Dod, Dodbury, Brown Dod, Great Dod, Dodd, Little Dodd, Starling Dodd.

doire-darach, Gaelic, 'oak-copse,' might be the source of Durdar.

dôl, Welsh, 'river-side meadow.' A British word corresponding to this is the first element of *Dollerline*.

dornach, Gaelic, 'pebbly.' A British equivalent of this is the second element of Cardurnock.

doup, northern dialect word of Norse origin, 'a rounded cavity, hollow bottom,' occurs occasionally in field-names, cf. Doup in Whicham.

draught, from early ME draht. The first occurrence of this word in NED in the sense 'a place where a net is drawn for fish' is dated

1895, though the word is recorded in the 13th century for the action of drawing the net. There are several occurrences in field and minor names, one of them (in Rockcliffe) dating from about 1234.

*dreg, ON, 'portage.' Drigg. This would be a mutated form of ON drag, which occurs in the sense 'steep slope' in Dundraw.

dropping, ME, here equivalent to *dripping*. Dropping Crag.

druim, Gaelic, 'ridge.' (*b*) Drumleaning. The British equivalent of drum, OWelsh, 'ridge,' occurs in Drumburgh, Dundraw.

drȳge, OE, 'dry.' Drayrigg, Dry Beck, Dryburn, Dry Stone Knott.

dub, a northern dialect word of uncertain origin, meaning 'a muddy or stagnant pool, a deep dark pool in a river,' is first recorded in NED in the early 16th century. It occurs in Dub Beck (2), Dubmill Point, Dubwath, *Dubwath*, *Aldelathedub*, with several forms from the 13th century. It is also fairly frequent in field-names.

dubh, Gaelic, 'black.' (*a*) Glen Dhu (*v.* gleann *infra*); (*c*) Curdiff. Cardew may have a British equivalent as second element.

dūn, OE, 'hill.' Dumblar Rigg (?), Snowden Close.

dún, Gaelic, 'hill.' Dunmallard Hill.

duru, OE, 'door, pass.' Dore Head, Lodore. This and/or the synonymous OE dor occurs also in field and minor names.

dwfr, Welsh, 'stream.' The British equivalent of this is the second element of Calder.

dyande, ODan, 'marsh, swamp.' Dian Ho.

dýr, ON, 'deer.' Dyrah.

ēa, OE, 'river.' Eamont, Caldew.

ēast, OE, 'east.' Easton (2), Holme East Waver.

efwr, Welsh, 'cow-parsnip.' *Caraverick*.

(ī)eg, OE, 'island.' Corney, *Hougenai*. Also in field-names. The synonymous (ī)egland occurs in Island Cottages.

eign, ON, 'holding.' *Aynthorfin* (?).

eik, ON, 'oak.' Aigill Sike, Aiketgate, Aikhead, Aikshaw, Aikton, *Aykcrist*, *Aykeland*, Eagle Gill, Haytongate, Crookdake, Lyzzick Hall. *Akegile* occurs also in the field-names of Flimby. The element is often difficult to distinguish from the northern development of OE āc.

einn, ON, 'one, alone.' Anthorn, *Ayntrepot*.

einstapi, ON, 'bracken.' Ainstable.

eithin, Welsh, 'furze.' A British word corresponding to this might be the second element of *Lanrekaythin*.

elri, ON, 'alders, place overgrown with alders.' Ellerbank, Eller Beck (3), Ellerbeck, Ellercarr Bridge, Ellergill Beck, Ellershaw Plantation, Ellerton. Ellers occurs a number of times as a minor name for which only late forms are available.

ende, OE, 'end.' Croftend (2), Townend, Town End, Waterend, West End, Woodend (2), Wood End. The corresponding ON **endi** occurs in Watendlath.

eng, ON, 'pasture, grassland.' *Flashinge Dykes*, Pyeing Fm, Skelling. Ing is very common in modern field-names.

Engla, OE, 'of the Angles.' Inglewood Forest.

ēowu, OE, 'ewe.' Ewanrigg, Yewbarrow.

erg, ON, a loanword from Irish *airigh*, 'shieling, hill pasture.' (*a*) Berrier, Birker, Cleator, Crookley Beck, Glaramara, Helewynherge (?), Hewer Hill, Mosser, *Ranerthwate*, Rannerdale, *Ravenerhals*, Salter, Stephney, Stockdalewath, Winder (2); (*b*) Langley.

ermite, ME from OFr, 'hermit.' *Armat Gill* (earlier name of Swinsty Gill), Armathwaite (3), Armboth (?), Arment Ho (?), Beckermet (?). Cf. also *Hermitebec* c. 1210 in Upper Denton fields.

eski, ON, 'ash.' Ashgill, Ashness, Eskrigg, Hesket (2), White Esk.

ewe, OFr, 'water,' has replaced ēa as the second element of Caldew.

eyrr, ON, 'bank or spit of sand or gravel.' Aira Beck, Arrowthwaite. Also in field-names.

fæger, OE, 'fair.' Fairhill.

fāg, OE, 'variegated.' Fawcettlees.

fal(o)d, OE, 'fold.' Faulds. Fauld and Fold are common among modern field-names.

f(e)alh, OE, 'fallow land.' Faugh. Faugh is common also among field-names.

fall, OE and ON, 'forest clearing,' or **falle**, ME, 'slope,' may be the first element of Fawepark.

Fan. Fanciful field and minor names can be divided into four main groups—nicknames denoting fertility or unfertility, names of foreign places, and names referring to sticky soil.

Among uncomplimentary names, the most frequent is Hunger or Hungry Hill, which occurs over half-a-dozen times. There are also several Hunger Riggs, one *Hungerhowe* and one Hungry Moor. The forms date from the 13th century onwards. Other names of this type are Bedlam Holme (Staffield, probably denoting land only madmen would farm), Beggaram Meadow (Dalston), Hard work (Corney), Hopeless meadow (Bootle), Misfortune field (Hesket), and Skinny Flint (Bootle).

Complimentary nicknames are Busy bitt (Little Clifton), Busy Yokeing (Bewcastle), Butterhill (Bewcastle), Butter Gills and Hill (Hutton-in-the-Forest), Easyfitt (Langwathby), Goodie (Bromfield), Mount Pleasant (Millom and Wetheral), Paradise (Bowness and Crosby-on-Eden).

American place-names seem popular as field-names: cf. America Plantation (Kirkbampton), America Wood (St Cuthbert Without),

Bunkers Hill (Dacre) and probably Brunkers Hill (Corney), California (Skirwith) and Carolina and Claremont (Gosforth). Other names of this type are Corsica, Flanders, French Flat and Waterloo (all in Dalston), Dunkirk (Alston), Jericho and Jordan Beck (both in Holme St Cuthbert), Leipsic and Moscow (both in Alston), *Ireland feild* (1597 in Hesket), Nineveh Wood (Kirkandrews Middle) and another Waterloo (Ulpha). The reference is often to a place on the outskirts of a parish. Other names denoting remote position are Come by Chance (Brampton) and Seldom Seen (Alston).

Names referring to sticky soil mostly contain *honey*. There are over half-a-dozen Honey Pots, and one Honey Croft. Glue Pot occurs in Crosby-on-Eden. Cf. also Pudding Crook (Askerton) and Pudding How (Dean). Pastry Crust (Hutton-in-the-Forest) may also refer to the texture of the soil.

Apart from these main groups, Three Cocked Hat (Irthington) refers to the shape of the field, and the precise significance of Ink Pot Meadow (Whicham), Jack-a-Dandy Hill, Harmless-Hill and Scab'dhill (Whitehaven), *Petticote* (1578 in Eskdale), *Salt seller* (1578 in Above Derwent), True Love Lands (Greystoke), Turn Out (Broughton) and Whale Jaws[1] (Bowness) is uncertain.

Folly, a name for an extravagant or foolish building (*v.* PN Wa 382–5), occurs fairly frequently in field and minor names. The forms are late.

fearn, OE, 'fern.' Farlam (?).

féhús, ON, 'cattle-shed.' (*a*) Fusehill Ho, Fewsteads (a field-name in Alston); (*c*) Yottenfews.

feld, OE, 'open country.' (*a*) Albyfield, Broadfield, Broad Field, Bromfield, Broomfield, Crossfield, Dykesfield, Gillfield Plantation, Itonfield, Millfield Wood, Sandsfield, Scalefield Gill Plantation, Southerfield, *Ureby Field*, Westfield Ho; (*b*) Blunderfield (?), Eaglesfield, Thurstonfield. Occurs *passim* in field-names, where it will have usually the later sense of the modern *field*, 'enclosed piece of land.'

fell, fiall, ON, 'fell, mountain.' (*a*) The Fell, Fell Close, Black Fell, Blaze Fell, Bolton Fell, Brae Fell, Caldbeck Fells, Cold Fell, Derwent Fells, *Fendesfell*, Harter Fell, Kirk Fell, Mell Fell, Newbiggin Fell, Sca Fell, Soulby Fell, Souther Fell, Staffield, Whinfell, Whin Fell; (*b*) Blunderfield (?). Common in field-names.

fenekel, ME, 'fennel,' or dialect **fenkel**, 'corner, bend,' may be the first element of Finkle St.

fenn, OE, 'fen.' Fenton.

fēond, OE, 'fiend.' *Fendesfell*.

[1] Probably the jaws were set up at the entrance to the field.

fēower, OE, 'four.' Fowrass. Cf. also *le Fourstanes* (1383), a field-name in Dearham, *the fower stonnes* (1589) in Rockcliffe and *Fourhowe* (1368) in Stanwix.

ferme, OFr, 'rent.' Farmlands.

(en)fermerie, OFr, '(monastic) infirmary.' Farmery (?).

finn, later **fionn**, Gaelic, 'white.' Fingland (?).

fit, ON, 'meadow.' (*a*) Fitz, The Fitz, Coldfitz Wood, Lambfoot; (*b*) *Fit Brandan*. Very common in field-names.

flasshe, **flosshe**, ME, 'pool, marshy place.' The Flosh, Flosh Gate. Common in field-names.

flat, ME (a loan word from ON *flǫt*), 'a level piece of ground.' (*a*) Flat Bank, Flatt Ho, Flaska, Fluskew, Hallflat, *Marshalflate*; (*b*) Brightenflat. Common in field-names.

Flemynge, ME, 'of the Flemings.' Flimby.

flēot, OE, **fljót**, ON, 'creek, inlet, estuary, stream,' occurs in field-names and in minor names for which only late forms are available. Cf. Cold Fleet Close, a modern field-name in Broughton, and Fleetwith, a minor name in Buttermere.

fles, ON, 'green spot among bare fells.' *Flashinge Dykes*.

flesja, ON, 'slab, flat stone.' Fleswick Bay.

fog, ME, 'rough grass.' Foggythwaite. Occurs also in field-names.

ford, OE, 'ford.' Blackford, Gosforth, *Hetherford*, *Rutterforde*. Also in field-names.

forest, ME from OFr, 'forest.' (*b*) Nicholforest.

forn, ON, 'old.' Foxley Henning, Thornby. In Thornby the word may be used as a personal name.

fors, ON, 'waterfall.' Hall Foss. Common in field and minor names.

fossa, Latin, 'ditch.' Monk Foss.

fōt, OE, **fótr**, ON, 'foot.' *Cumelkeldfot*, *Elnefoot* (earlier name of Maryport), *Irthyngfote*, *Rauenesgilfot*. *Foot* and *Head* (OE hēafod) are very common indeed in minor names, denoting the upper and lower ends of something, cf. e.g. Wallfoot and Wallhead in Stanwix, and the common Lonning Foot and Lonning Head. There are medieval forms for a fair number of these names, but for the majority the forms are 16th century or later. fōt is commonly used of land at the mouth of a river or stream, and hēafod occasionally of a river source.

frēre, ME from OFr, 'friar.' Friargate.

fugol, OE, 'bird.' *Foulwood*.

fūl, OE, 'dirty,' is fairly frequent in field-names and in minor names for which there are only late forms. 'Foul sike,' 'foul bridge' and 'foul ford' are names which occur several times.

fyrhþ(e), OE, 'wood.' *Frithebec*. Occurs also in field-names, where modern Frith is fairly frequent.

gærs, græs, OE, 'grass.' Grassgarth, Kershope (?). ON **gres** is the first element of Grassoms. **gærstūn**, OE, 'grassy enclosure,' occurs once as a field-name in Irton.

gafl, ON, 'gable.' Gavel Fell, Great Gable, Green Gable.

g(e)alga, OE, 'gallows.' Gallowbarrow, Gallowberry, Gallowhow, Gallows Hill, Gillalees (?). Among the field-names there are *Galberghfeld* (1354), *Gallobergh, Gallowbargh* (1568) in Carlisle and Lazonby, *Gallowhills* (1619 and 1764) in Penrith and Dalston and a modern Gallows field in Ulpha and Gallows Bank in Millom. ON **galgi** is a probable first element of Galley Gill, Galligill and Galleywreay.

gap, ON, 'break or opening in a range of mountains,' occurs in several minor names for which only late forms are available. There is one early occurrence (13th century) in the field-names of St Bees.

gāra, OE, 'triangular piece of land,' occurs occasionally in field-names, several times in the compound **garbrade**.

garbrad(e), ME. In other counties surveyed *garbrode* is a common medieval field-name, denoting a broad strip of land tapering to a point. This compound (from **gāra** and **brād**) is the source of *le Garbrad* (1303 Ellenborough), *Garbrades* (c. 1240 Irthington), *Garebrad* (1261 Rottington). There are also fields called *garbredes* (1530 Carlisle), *Garbreads* (1568 Lazonby), *Garbreade* (1619 Great Salkeld), which may contain OE **brǣd**, 'broad strip of land,' or may owe the vowel in the second element to the northern dialect development of ME *ā*.

garðr, ON, 'enclosure.' (*a*) Garthfolds, Guardhouse, Calfgarth Plantation, Crewgarth, Dalegarth, Driggith Beck, Fishgarth Holm, Grassgarth, Monkgarth, *Scoggarbar*, Stonegarthside, Temple Garth, Westgarth, Westgarth-hill; (*c*) Snittlegarth. Occurs *passim* in field-names, where the modern forms Garth and G(u)ard are both common. In field-names, as in Fishgarth and Monkgarth *supra*, it frequently refers to an enclosure in a river for catching fish.

gāt, OE, 'goat.' Gatesgarth.

gata, ON, 'road.' Burrowgate, Corbygates, Friargate, Gossipgate, Hagget End, Haytongate, *Holegatebeck*, Howgate Cottage, Sandgate, Shaddongate. It occurs in a number of street and other minor names for which there are only late forms, and in some lost street names.

gate, ME, used apparently in the modern northern dialect sense, 'the right or privilege of pasture for cattle.' Bleagate.

gauð, ON, 'barking.' Gowder Crag.

gavel, northern dialect word meaning 'strip of land,' is the probable source of the element *gavel* which occurs in the field-names of Dundraw, Hesket (1650), Holm Cultram (1538) and Kirkandrews upon Eden.

geafol, OE, 'fork' (in this case of a river). *Will Ave* (?).

geat, OE, 'gate.' (*a*) Aiketgate, Barrass Gate, Beck Gate, Caldewgate, Highgate (2), Parkgate; (*b*) Botchergate, Rickergate. Occurs also in field-names, where Yate is a frequent modern form.

geil, ON, 'ravine, cleft' and 'narrow path.' Gale Hall, Scalegill Hall (?), Skelgill. Also in field-names.

geilt, OIr, 'madman, wild man.' Gelt (?).

geit, ON, 'goat.' Gatesgarth, Gatesgill.

gil, ON, 'ravine, narrow valley.' (*a*) Gill (3), Gill Beck, Gill Bridge, Gillfield Plantation, Gillfoot, Gillhead, Gill Ho, Aigill Sike, *Armat Gill*, Ashgill, Baxton Gill, *Bigryggyll*, Blagill, Bleaberry Gill, *Brangull*, Catgill Hall, Cavel Gill, Eagle Gill, Hazel Gill, Heggle Sike, Hethersgill, Hole Gill, *Holgil*, Holghyll, Howgill (2), Illgill Head, Ivegill, Kidburngill, Millgill, Nattrass Gill, North Gill, Priestgill, Scale Gill, Scalegill Hall (?), Scar Gill, *Scraithegil*, Sickergill, Skelgill, Stargill, Stotgill, Swarthgill, Worm Gill; (*b*) Gillcambon, *Gillefinchor*, Gilgarran, Aiglegill, Davygill, Garrigill, *Rauenesgil*, Ravensgill Plantation, Sunnygill Beck; (*c*) Petter Gill. The word occurs *passim* in field-names. Its frequent use as the second element of a stream-name is responsible for the etymology of Gilsland (2–3) mentioned by Camden: "*Gillesland*..., quæ regiuncula est impedita torrentibus, unde nomen (torrentes enim *Gilles* vocant)" (W. Camden, *Britannia*, p. 526. London 1587).

gildri, ON, 'trap, snare.' Gilderdale Forest, *Gilderskugh*, *Gilderstanflat*.

glas, ME, 'glass.' *Glashouses*. This compound also occurs more than once as a field-name.

glas, Welsh, 'grey.' The corresponding British word occurs in Clesketts (?), Glasson.

gleann, Gaelic, 'glen.' Glen Dhu. The name may, however, be British, corresponding to ModW *glyndu*, spelt in a pseudo-Gaelic way.

gliúfr, ON, 'ravine.' Glaramara.

gol(a), ON, 'wind.' Gowbarrow (?).

gōs, OE, 'goose.' *Goseterne*, Gosforth.

gossib, ME, 'person with whom one has contracted affinity according to canon law.' Gossipgate.

gote, dialect word meaning 'watercourse,' is fairly common in field and minor names. Cf. Goat in Hutton Soil and Papcastle, *old gote wathe*, 1589 in Rockcliffe.

grǣg, OE, 'grey.' This occurs most frequently in the name Graystone, which is one of the commonest minor names in the county. Graystone, Gray Stone, Gray Stones, Graystone Ho, Greason Cottage (?), Greystone, Greystone Cottages survive on the map, and the name has also been noted as that of a field in the parishes of Alston, Bewcastle, Blindcrake, Broughton, Castle Carrock, Little Clifton, Dalston, Dean, Ellenborough, Glassonby, Muncaster, St John's, Warwick, Wetheral, Workington and Wreay. Cloven Stone in Eskdale is *the cloven gray stone* in 1587.

grange, ME from OFr, 'grange.' Grange (2), Grange Bridge, Grange Fm.

grein, ON, 'division, branch, fork,' used of a small valley opening from another or of the meeting-place of two streams, occurs in a number of minor names for which the forms available are 16th century or later. Cf. Grainsgill Beck, *Grane beck* (early name of Wiley Gill), Grain Gill in Eskdale and High and Low Grains in Askerton. Modern Grain, Grayne are frequent in field-names.

grēne, OE, 'green.' The Green, Green Rigg, Greenrigg, Greenup Edge, Greenwell. **grœnn**, ON, 'green.' Greenah (2), Green How, Greenside, Green Side. Also in field-names.

grēot, OE, 'gravel.' Greathill Beck. **griót**, ON, 'gravel.' Greta.

gríss, ON, 'young pig.' Grise Beck, Mungrisdale.

grið, OE, 'truce, sanctuary.' *Grith Cross.*

gróf, ON, 'pit.' *Petegroves.*

groyne, ModE, 'a defensive sea wall.' Grune Ho and Point.

gwragedd, Welsh, 'women.' A British equivalent occurs in *Raswraget.*

(ge)hæg, OE, **haye**, ME, 'enclosure,' occurs in *Thueitdounegaleg'* and the early forms for Plumpton Wall and Botlands Blawith.

***hær**, OE, 'stone.' Harras (452).

hæsel, OE, 'hazel.' Hazelspring, Hazelrigg. **hesli**, ON, 'hazel.' Hazel Gill, Hazel Sike. Occasionally in field-names.

hafn, ON, 'harbour.' Whitehaven.

hafoc, OE, or **haukr**, ON, 'hawk.' Hawksdale. The word may be used as a personal name.

hafri, ON, 'oats.' Harberry Beck, Haverigg.

hagi, ON, 'enclosure.' Dyrah.

haining, ME, 'enclosure.' Haining Bank, Hainings Gate, Hinning Ho (2), Foxley Henning.

h(e)alh, OE, 'corner, recess, (secret) place,' the source of northern dialect *haugh*, 'a piece of flat alluvial land by the side of a river.' The latter is usually the sense of h(e)alh in north country place-names. (*a*) Haile, Ameshaugh, Edenhall, Strenshal, Wetheral; (*b*) Isel; (*c*) Lessonhall. *haugh* occurs in modern field-names.

h(e)all, OE, 'hall.' Hall Bank (2), Hall Beck, Hallflat, Hallsteads (2), Hallthwaites, Blackhall, Cardew Hall, Fleming Hall, Kirkland Hall, Lamonby Hall, Lazonby Hall, Netherhall, Prior Hall, *Randerside Hall*, Uldale Hall, Warwick Hall, White Hall, Wood Hall, Woodhall (2).

hals, ON, 'neck, col.' *Edderlanghals*, Esk Hause, *Ravenerhals*.

hām, OE, 'village, estate, manor, homestead.' (*a*) Hames Hall, Brigham, Dearham, Farlam (?), Holm Cultram, Queen's Hames; (*c*) Sebergham. *v.* also -ingahām *infra*.

hār, OE, 'grey' or 'boundary.' Harrop Tarn (?). Hare Stone(s) occurs as a modern name in Caldbeck and Wetheral.

hara, OE, 'hare.' Haresceugh, Harras, Harrop Tarn (?).

harðr, ON, 'hard.' Hard Knott.

haugr, ON, 'hill, mound.' (*a*) How, Howes, How Hall, Hewer Hill, *Hougenai*, Howscales, *Arneshowe*, Blencow, Bracken How, Brotto, Calfhow Pike, Calva Hall, Calvo, Cargo, Cleahall, Cony Hill, *Cuningishow*, Fowrass, Gallow How, Greenah (2), Green How, Hallsenna, *Lauerdeshou*, Leashore, Lowsay, Lynehow, Mealo Ho, Picket How, Prior How, *Serganteshou*, Shundraw, Skelda, Stone How, Stony How (?), *Thuahovel*, Ulpha, Whelpo, Winnow; (*b*) Feather Knott, Pardshaw, *Tostihow*; (*c*) Ravelsaye Ho, Skiddaw. Common in field-names.

haut, OFr, 'high.' Haltcliff Hall (?).

hēafod, OE, 'head, headland.' (*a*) Heads Wood, Aikhead, Bennethead, Birkett Beck, Birkett Mire, Bolton Head, Crossgill Head, Hartside Height, Hesket Fm, Hesket Newmarket, High Head Castle, Kinniside, Kirkhead, Latrigg, Latterhead, Raughtonhead, Sparket, Swinside, Thiefside Hill, Townhead; (*c*) Armaside. Fairly common in field-names. *v.* **fōt** *supra*.

hearg, OE, 'heathen temple.' Harras (169), Harrow Head.

*hedr, Welsh, feminine of **hydr**, 'strong.' A British equivalent may be the source of Hether Burn.

hēg, OE, 'hay.' Hagget End, Haithwaite, Hayborough, Haythwaite, Hayton (2).

hē(a)h, OE, 'high.' Heggle Sike (?), High Head Castle, High Ireby, Highlaws, High Lodore, Highmoor. Also in field-names.

hē(a)hdēor, OE, 'tall deer.' Hethersgill, *Hetherford*.

h(i)elde, OE, 'slope.' Laithwaite. Occurs also in field-names. This compound with **hlaða** occurs as a field-name in Clifton.

heorot, OE, 'hart.' Harelaw Hill, Harker, Hartlaw, Hartrigg, Hartside Height, Hartley Burn.

hestr, ON, 'stallion, horse.' Eastholme Ho, Hestham, *Hestholm*. **hest-skeið**, 'race-course.' Hesket in the Forest.

hey, ON, 'hay.' Blennerhasset.

hjól, ON, 'wheel.' Shoulthwaite.

hjǫrtr, ON, 'hart.' Harter Fell.

hlāford, OE, 'lord.' *Lauerdeshou*, Lord's Seat.

hlaða, ON, 'barn.' Laithes, Laythes, Laithwaite, *Aldelathedub*, Aldoth, Newlaithes Hall, Silloth. Modern Lathe, Leath, are quite common in field-names.

hlāw, OE, 'hill, mound, tumulus.' Great Blacklaw Hill, Dumblar Rigg (?), Harelaw Hill, Highlaws, Merelaw Hill.

hlidgeat, OE, 'swing gate,' occurs occasionally in field and minor names: cf. *Lidyate*, c. 1260 in Upper Denton, Leadgate in Alston.

hlíð, ON, 'slope.' Ainstable, Leath Ward.

hlōse, OE, 'pig-sty.' Lostrigg Beck (?), Lowsay (?). Occasionally in field-names.

Hlȳde, an OE stream-name derived from *hlūd*, 'loud.' Liddel Water.

hlynn, OE, 'torrent.' Croglin.

***hobb(e)**, OE, 'hummock' (postulated by Ekwall, Studies² 177–8, as the first element of Hautbois Nf). (*b*) Hobcarton (?).

hofuð, ON, 'head.' High Scawdel, *Houtbergh* (?), Stangrah, *Swarthow*, Whitehaven.

hogg, ON, 'right of cutting trees or turf.' Modern hag(g) is frequent in field and minor names.

hōh, OE, 'projecting ridge of land.' (*a*) Hewthwaite Hall, *Hothwait*, Houghton, Howthwaite, Hutton, Cannerheugh, Cloffocks, Moota Hill, The Spillers (?), Stoddah, Torpenhow, Wodow Bank; (*c*) Cordamoss. Also in field-names.

holegn, OE, 'holly,' occurs frequently in field and minor names, usually in the form Hollin. All the forms are late.

holh, **hol**, OE, **hol**, **holr**, ON, noun and adjective, 'hole, hollow.' The OE element occurs in Hollowdyke Fm, Toddell, Todholes. The ON is in *Holebech*, Hole Beck, *Holegatebeck*, Holghyll, *Holgil*, Hole Gill, How Beck, Howgate Cottage, Howgill (2). Occasionally in field-names; there is another *Holgil* in Eskdale and Wasdale.

hóll, ON, 'isolated hill.' Staffield, Ward Hall and minor names (249).

holmr, ON, 'islet,' used of any piece of land isolated from its surroundings, such as a piece of dry land in a fen, a piece of land partly surrounded by a stream. (*a*) Holme Abbey, Holmhead, Holme Ho, Holme Lane, Holmrook, Ambrose Holme, Battail Holme, Brigham, Brundholme, Burtholme, Eastholme Ho, Grassoms, Hestham, *Hestholm*, *Langholm*, Lawrenceholm, Lyneholme, Middleholm Moss, Millholme (2), *Respholm*, Rougholme, St Herbert's Island (earlier *Herbertholm*), Sleightholme, Studholme, Thornholme, Thrangholm, Wedholme Flow, Whiteholme; (*b*) Baldwinholme, Randalholm Hall, Willow Holme; (*c*) Julian Holme. Occurs *passim* in field-names.

hop, OE, 'piece of enclosed land in the midst of fens,' but generally occurring in place-names with the meaning 'a small enclosed valley, a smaller opening branching out from the main dale, a blind valley.' Burnhope Seat, Greenup Edge, Harrop Tarn, Kershope, *Meadhope*, Rotherhope, Wythop.

hors, OE, 'horse,' was probably the original first element of Rosley, but has been replaced by the equivalent ON **hross**. **hross** occurs also in Rosewain.

hrafn, ON, 'raven.' Rainsbarrow Wood (the element may be used as a personal name), Rannerdale, *Ranerthwate, Ravenerhals*.

hrēod, OE, 'reed.' Reathwaite, Redhill, Redmire. *Re(e)dmire* or *Readmire* occurs also as a field-name in Aikton, Blennerhasset, Caldbeck, Eskdale, Hesket in the Forest, Staffield, Watermillock and Westward. Cf. *Readmore* (1625) in Lazonby and *Redeker* (1322), *Redekare* (1323), a compound of **hrēod** and **kiarr**, in the field-names of St John Beckermet.

hreysi, ON, 'cairn, heap of stones.' (*a*) Racy Cott, Harras; (*b*) Dunmail Raise. Also in field-names.

hrīs, OE, 'brushwood.' (*a*) *Rysebrigge*; (*c*) Nattrass.

hrycg, OE, **hryggr**, ON, 'ridge.' Biggrigg, Birkrigg, Brackenrigg, Brackenriggs, Brownrigg (3), Castlerigg, Cast Rigg, Dockrayrigg Ho, Dumblar Rigg, Eskrigg, Ewanrigg, Finglandrigg, Greenrigg(2), Green Rigg, Hartrigg, Haverigg, Hazelrigg, Langrigg, Layriggs, Loughrigg, Mealrigg, Millrigg, Orton Rigg, Oxenriggs, Scalesrigg, Shaw Rigg, Skiprigg, Wetheriggs, Wheyrigg, Whitrigg (3), Whitriggs (2). One list has been made for the OE and ON elements, as there are a number of names in which either of them could equally well be present. They occur frequently in field-names.

hryding, OE, 'clearing, cleared land.' Ridding, Riddings, Rudding, The Ruddings. Ridding, Rudding, Reading are common in field and minor names.

hrȳðer, OE, 'cattle.' *Rutterforde*, Rotherhope.

hulfere, ME, 'holly.' Hullerbank, *Hulverbosk, Hulverhirst*.

hunda-sveinn, ON, 'dog-keeper.' Hunsonby (?).

hūs, OE, 'house.' (*a*) Uzzicar, *Glashouses*, Millhouse, Monkhouse, Moor Ho, Moorhouse (2), Newsham, Salthouse, Scugger Ho, Stone Ho, *Woodhouse*; (*b*) Nealhouse. **hús**, ON, 'house.' Guardhouse, Holme Ho. Also in field-names, where *House-stead* occurs several times.

hvelpr, ON, 'whelp.' Whelpo.

hvǫnn, ON, 'Angelica archangelica.' Wanthwaite (?).

hwæte, OE, or **hveiti**, ON, 'wheat.' Whitecroft Bridge.

hwamm, OE, **hvammr**, ON, 'marshy hollow.' Midgeholme (?). *Wham* occurs occasionally in modern field-names.

*hwēoling, OE, 'with wheels.' Whillimoor Foot.

hwīt, OE, 'white.' Whitbarrow Hall, White Hall. **hvítr**, ON, 'white.' Whitbeck, White Esk, Whitehaven, Whiteholme, Whitelyne. Either the OE or the ON word may be the first element of Whitrigg (2), Whitriggs (3). They occur also in field-names.

hwyrfel, OE, **hvirfill**, ON, 'circle.' Possibly in Hurlbarrow, Wharrels Hill, Whorl Gill. The forms are late, however, and **quarrel** (*infra*) is a possible alternative for Wharrels Hill and Whorl Gill.

hyll, OE, 'hill.' The Hill, Hillfield, Hill Head, Boustead Hill, Bracken Hill (2), Brackenhill Tower, Cambeckhill, Coathill, Greathill Beck, High Bankhill, Redhill, *Stubhill*, Thorn Hill, Warnell (?). Frequent in field-names.

-hylte, OE, 'wood.' Salkeld.

hyrne, OE, 'corner,' occurs in field-names.

hyrst, OE, 'hillock, bank, wooded eminence, wood.' Bannest Hill, Birkhurst, Burthinghurst, Crookhurst, Hardest, Hazelhurst, *Hulverhirst*, Long Hurst, Swallowhurst. Common in field-names.

hysse, OE, probably meaning a kind of water plant. Hycemoor.

hȳð, OE, 'port, haven, landing place on a river.' Hyton.

iâl, Welsh, 'fertile upland region.' A corresponding British word may be the second element of Tindale Tarn, Tindale Fell and *Tyneelside*.

ífa, ON, 'yew stream.' Ive (?).

ille, ME from ON, 'evil.' Illgill Head.

impe, OE, 'young plant,' and the compound **impgarth** 'enclosure for young plants (possibly osiers),' occur occasionally in field-names, cf. *Ympegard*, c. 1250 in Farlam.

infield and **outfield**, used in the north of 'arable land which receives manure and is perpetually in crop' and 'arable land not kept in manure at some distance from the farm-stead; outlying inferior land,' occur occasionally in field and minor names. There are early examples of both terms in Tallentire (c. 1260).

-inga, OE, genitive of **-ingas**, meaning, when used in combination with a topographical term, 'the dwellers at,' may be the middle element of Arrowthwaite. **-ingahām**, OE, 'hām of the people of —,' occurs in Addingham, Hensingham, Whicham. **-ingatūn**, OE, 'tūn of the people of —,' may be contained in Frizington. **-ingtūn**, OE, '—'s tūn,' occurs in Cumwhitton, Distington (?), Frizington (?), Harrington, Rottington, Workington.

innam, **innom** and **inhoke**, ME, both meaning 'a piece of land taken in, or enclosed,' the latter being applied to an enclosure for cultivation of part of the fallow land, occur occasionally in field-names. **intak**, ME, 'an enclosure from the waste,' is very frequent in field and minor names.

ír, Welsh, 'fresh, green.' A derivative of a corresponding British word may be contained in Irt, Irthing.

íra, ON, 'of the Irishmen.' Ireby.

Iscā, a British river-name on which see RN 151–6, is the source of Esk.

Itunā, British, a river-name possibly cognate with Sanskrit *pitú-*, 'sap.' Eden (?).

īw, OE, 'yew.' Yew Bank.

ká, ON, 'jackdaw.' Caber.

kaldr, ON, 'cold.' Caldbeck, Cald Beck, Caud Beck, Coldfitz Wood.

*karlatún, ON, 'farm of the free men or peasants.' The name is not found in Scandinavia, and Ekwall (DEPN) suggests that Carl(e)ton is likely in most cases to be due to Scandinavianisation of OE *Ceorlatūn*. Carlatton (?), Carleton (4).

kaupaland, or a variant kaupuland, ON, 'bought land.' Copeland.

kavli, ON, 'cylindrical stake.' Cavel Gill.

kelda, ON, 'spring, deep water-hole, smooth-flowing stream.' (a) Kelbarrow, Kellbank, Kelsick, Kelton, Blind Keld, *Cumelkeldfot*, Threlkeld, *Wytheskeld*; (b) Keldhouse Bridge, Dunningwell (earlier *Duningekeld*), Simon Kell. Frequent in field-names.

kerling, ON, 'old woman.' *Kerlingsik* (field-name in Gosforth). Possibly the first element of Carling Knott and Carling Stone.

kiarr, ON, 'marsh.' Ellercarr Bridge, Harker, Selker. Occurs in field-names.

*kikall, ON, 'winding,' or the compound Kykla, a Norwegian river-name meaning 'winding stream,' is the source of Keekle.

kirkja, ON, 'church.' The nominative is found in Kirkandrews (3), Kirkbampton, Kirkbride, *Kirkbrynnok*, Kirkcambeck, Kirkhead, Kirklinton, Kirkoswald, Kirksanton, *Kyrklayne* (a lost street-name in Penrith), Bridekirk, Islekirk. The genitive, kirkju, occurs in Curthwaite (2), Kirkbank, Kirk Beck (2), Kirkeby, *Kirkeby Crossan*, *Kirkebi Johannis*, Kirk Fell, Kirkland (3). Cf. also the early forms for St Bees. There are some instances of the name Kirkland for which only late forms are available.

klettr, ON, 'rock, cliff.' Cleator.

klif, ON, 'cliff.' Rockcliffe.

klint, clint, presumably from Dan klint, 'rock,' occurs quite frequently in field and minor names, but all the forms are late. Cf. Coombs Clint in Ainstable.

knott, ON, cnotta, late OE, 'a rocky hill or summit.' (a) Knott, Knotts; (b) *Editheknot*. There are several occurrences of Knott(s) in field and minor names. In Dry Stone Knott the sense is presumably 'heap of stones,' as in *Sir Gawain and the Green Knight* 1431 ff.

knútr, ON, 'knot, craggy hill.' Hard Knott.

konungr, ON, 'king.' *Cuningishow*.

korki, ON, 'oats.' Corby (?).

kráka, ON, 'crow.' Cracrop (?). Also in field-names.

kringla, ON, 'circle.' High Crindledike, Crindledyke, Cringle-thwaite Terrace. Cf. also *Crengale*, 1346 in Westnewton.

krókr, ON, 'crook, bend.' (*a*) Crook Burn, Crookdale, Crook Gill, Crookhurst, Crookley Beck, Crookwath, Holmrook (?); (*c*) Froddle Crook. Occurs also in field-names. ME **crōk**, from **krókr**, is probably the first element of Croglin. In modern minor names *Crook* is very frequently used in combination with a river-name.

kross, ON, 'cross.' Crosby-on-Eden, Crosscanonby, Crossdale (2), Crosthwaite, Allerby.

kum(b)l, ON, 'grave mound, cairn.' *Cumelkeldfot* (?).

kví, ON, 'fold.' Wheyrigg.

lacu, OE, 'stream, watercourse.' Arlecdon.

Lady, probably used in the names of pieces of land dedicated to the service of Our Lady (PN Wa 335), occurs about a dozen times in field-names, with various second elements of which **land** is the most common. Cf. *Marydykes* 1859 in Staffield.

læs, OE, 'pasture, meadow-land.' (*a*) Lees Hill, Cardewlees, Fawcett-lees, Whitrigglees; (*c*) Blitterlees. The forms are all late. Common in field-names.

lagán, Gaelic, 'hollow.' Logan Beck, *Catlogan*. Occurs occasionally in field-names.

lágr, ON, from which is derived **lāh**, ME, 'low.' Occurs in Lodore, Low Ireby.

lain, ME, occurs occasionally in field-names: cf. *branden layne gate*, 1589 in Greystoke, *the Crosse laine*, 1679 in Plumpton Wall, *the Long Layne*, 1604 in St John's. The exact sense of the term is unknown, but probably it denotes land which is periodically allowed to lie fallow by being sown in regular *lains* or divisions. The word may be the source of the field-name element *lion*, only found once in Cumberland (in Brampton), but more frequent in other counties. For further references *v*. PN W 439.

laking, ME, 'playing, amusement,' is probably the first element of Laiking Wood and Laking How.

lamb, OE, 'lamb.' Lambsceugh.

land, OE and ON, 'earth, soil, landed property, estate.' (*a*) Craglands Sike, Crosslands, Cumberland, Debateable Land, Kirkland (3), Longlands (2), Moorland Close, Newlands (5), Sunderland, Threapland; (*b*) Gilsland; (*c*) *Sokbrodland*. In field-names the word may have the technical sense 'strip of land in an open field.'

*landā, British, 'enclosure.' Lamplugh.

lane, OE, 'lane,' occurs occasionally in street-names. Cf. *le Kyrklayne*, 1493 in Penrith.

lang, OE, **langr**, ON, 'long.' Lambfoot, *Langholm*, Langrigg, Langthwaite, *Langthwaite*, Langwathby, Lanthwaite Green, Long Barrow, Long Bridge, Longburgh, Long Hurst, Longlands (2),

Long Moor, Long Strath, Longthwaite (3), Longtown, *Edder-langhals*. Also in field-names.

lapboard, presumably the modern dialect word meaning 'board on which tailors iron or press out their seams' used descriptively, occurs twice as a field-name.

later, probably from a Goidelic word meaning 'hill, slope,' represented in OIr *lettir*, Gaelic *leitir*. Latrigg, Latterhead, Whinlatter.

laufsær, ON, 'leafy lake.' Loweswater.

laukr, ON, 'garlic, leek.' Lacra, Loughrigg (?).

launde, ME from OFr *launde*, 'open space in woodland, glade, pasture,' occurs occasionally in field-names, and is the second element of the earliest form for Farmlands.

lāwerce, OE, 'lark,' is probably the first element of Laverickstone, but the forms are late: it occurs occasionally in field-names, cf. *Laverkewode* (1259 Askerton), *Layrocsyk* (c. 1203 Loweswater).

leac, Gaelic, 'slab stone, flat rock.' (b) *Lakewolf*.

lēactūn, OE, 'kitchen-garden.' Carlatton (?).

*lece, OE, 'brook.' Leakley (?).

ledy, ME, 'lady.' Catlowdy.

lē(a)h, OE, 'wood, open place in a wood, meadow, pasture land.' Bradley, Farlam (?), Hartley Burn, *Leakley*, Rosley, Stockley Bridge.

(s)leib-, 'to drip,' is suggested by Ekwall (RN 252) as the root to which the river-name Lyne belongs.

leikr, ON, 'play.' Ullock (2), Woolloaks.

leirr, ON, 'clay.' Lairthwaite, Layriggs. Frequent in field-names, a compound which occurs several times being *Larepotts* (1742 Workington and 1760 *et seq.* Dalston), *Leirpottes* (1355 *et seq.* Carlisle), *Layerpittrodes* (1568 Lazonby). Cf. *Clepot* ('clay pot'), 1343 in Caldbeck.

leysingr, ON, 'freedman.' Lazencastle Wood (?), Lazonby, *Cater-laising*. The word was often used as a personal name in the North of England, and this may be the case in any of these names.

līn, OE, **lín**, ON, 'flax.' Linedraw, Linethwaite, Linskeldfield, Linstock, Linewath. Also in field-names.

lind, OE and ON, 'lime tree.' Linbeck (2), Line Beck.

lítell, ON, 'little.' Little Dale. **lȳtel**, OE. Little Bampton, Little Blencow, Little Corby, Little Crosthwaite.

ljóss, ON, 'bright, shining.' Leashore, Liza, Lyzzick Hall.

llanerch, Welsh, 'glade.' A British word corresponding to this is the first element of Lanercost, Lanerton (?), *Lanrekaythin*.

llosg, Welsh, 'burning.' A British equivalent is probably found in Newton Arlosh.

loc(a), OE, 'enclosure,' is probably the second element of Ewelock, which occurs twice as a minor name, with only late forms.

lonning, ME, 'a lane, a by-road,' occurs *passim* in field and minor names, but all the forms are late. Lonning Foot and Lonning Head are very common.

lopt, ON, 'loft.' Lofshaw Hill (?), Losca (?), Lothwaite, Low Scales, Lowthwaite. There is another *Lofthayt* (c. 1230) in the field-names of Bromfield, and another *Loftskales* (1369) in the field-names of Above Derwent.

*lort, OE, 'dirt.' Lot Burn.

lown, northern dialect, 'quiet, sheltered,' possibly from ON *logn*. Longthwaite.

luh, OE, 'loch, pond.' Lough (3).

lundr, ON, 'grove, small wood.' Lund, Lund Bridge, *Aykelund*, Plumbland, Slealands.

lyng, ON, 'ling.' Lingclose, Lingcove Beck. Occurs in field-names.

mægden, OE, 'maiden.' Maiden Castle. **mæge**, OE, 'maiden.' Mawbray.

maen, Welsh, 'stone.' A British equivalent occurs in (*a*) Redmain, Triermain; (*c*) Temon.

(ge)mæne, OE, 'common,' occurs in field-names, and is the source of the common modern element Mean: cf. *meane inge*, 1578 in Ennerdale.

(ge)mære, OE, 'boundary.' Mere Beck (2), Merebeck Gill, Mere Gill (2), Meregill Beck, Merelaw Hill, Mere Sike, Wallmoorsike. *Meresik* and *Merebec* also occur twice as field-names, the former in Irthington and Dalston and the latter in Waterhead and Wigton, and Meer Stone occurs several times as a field-name.

mains, plural of northern dialect *main*, aphetic from *domain*, *demesne*, meaning 'demesne lands' or 'farm attached to a mansion house, home farm,' occurs frequently in field and minor names. Cf. *Maynes*, 1387 in Brampton.

mallacht, Gaelic, 'curses.' Dunmallard Hill (?).

manach, Gaelic, 'monk.' Scarrowmanwick (?).

maðra, ON, 'madder.' Matterdale.

mearc, OE, 'boundary.' March of Carlisle, The West March.

mede, ME, 'meadow.' Meadhope. ME *med(e)we*, from the oblique form of OE *mǣd*, occurs occasionally in field-names, cf. *Brademedowe* (1425) in Carlisle, *brode meadowes* (1589) in Farlam and *Le Brademedowe* (1442) in Skelton.

*meĭgh, 'to urinate,' ***meigh**, 'to drizzle,' are suggested by Ekwall (RN 295) as possible roots from which the river-name Mite has developed.

melr, ON, 'sandbank, dune.' Meles, Mealo Ho, Meolbank, Eskmeals.

mere, OE, 'pool.' Buttermere, Thirlmere.

micel, OE, **mikill**, ON, 'great, large.' Great Gable (earlier *Mykel-gavel*), Micklethwaite (the latter compound occurs again as a field-name in Millom).

middel, OE, 'middle.' Mealrigg, Middleholm Moss, Middle Moor, Middlesceugh, Middle Tongue, Millholme. Also in field-names.

moel, Welsh, 'bare hill.' A British equivalent of this is the source of Mell Fell, and a diminutive formed from the word is the second element of Watermillock.

*moldi, ON, 'top of the head,' used as a hill-name. (*b*) Mockerkin.

monadh, Gaelic, 'hill ground.' Kinmont.

*moniδ, Primitive Cumbric, 'mountain.' (*c*) Tarnmonath.

mōr, OE, 'moor, waste upland; fen.' The Moor, Moorend, Moor Ho, Moorhouse (3), Moorland Close, Moorside, Moorthwaite (2), Morton (2), Morton Sceugh, Murrah, Murthwaite Moor, Murton, Alston Moor, Broughton Moor, Burghmoor Ho, *Burntippet Moor*, Greystoke Moor, Highmoor, Hycemoor, Kingmoor, Long Moor, Middle Moor, Monk Moors, *Northmoor*, Seaton Moor, Whillimoor Foot. Also in field-names.

mos, OE, **mosi**, ON, 'moss, peat-bog.' Mosses, Moasdale, Mosedale, Mosedale Beck, Mosser, Mossthwaite, Blea Moss, *Cranberry Moss*, Normoss, Walton Moss. Frequent in field-names, and in minor names for which only late forms are available.

(ge)mōt, OE, 'meeting,' used in place-names of 'a junction of streams' and of 'an assembly, moot.' Moota Hill, Ameshaugh, Eamont.

mote, ME, 'mound.' The Mote, Liddel Strength (earlier *the Mote of Lydall*).

munuc, OE, 'monk.' Monk Foss, Monkgarth Pool, Monkhouse Hill, Monk Moors, Monks Dike, *Monkwath*. Cf. also *Monekewath*, 1279 in Workington.

mūs, OE, **mús**, ON, 'mouse.' Mousthwaite Comb (?).

mūþa, OE, 'mouth of a river, estuary.' Cockermouth.

mycg, OE, 'midge.' Midgeholme.

myln, OE, 'mill.' Millbeck (2), Millfield Wood, Millgill Bridge, Millholme, Millhouse, Millom, Millrigg, Milton, Denton Mill, Dubmill Point, Irthington Mill, Sparket Mill. Early references to windmills must be contained in the field-names *le Milnehull* (1303 in Ellenborough) and *Melnebergh* (1270 in Papcastle), *Milneberch'* (c. 1250 in Little Clifton).

mýrr, ON, 'swampy ground.' (*a*) Mirebank Wood, Mireside, Birkmere Wood, Birkmire, Braithmoor, Cardew Mires, Cleamire, Colmire Sough, Peatmoor Wood, Redmire, Starnmire, Thackmire; (*c*) Wragmire. Frequent in field-names.

nabbi, ON, 'projecting peak,' occurs several times in minor names for which there are only late forms. Cf. Nab End in Greystoke, Nabend in Watermillock, Birknab Wood in Matterdale and Nab Crags in St John's.

naddr, ON, 'point, wedge.' Naddle.

næs, OE, **nes**, ON, 'headland, cape.' Ashness, Bowness, Isthmus, Skinburness, Wrynose.

nant, Welsh, 'valley, brook.' A variant of the British word equivalent to this is probably the source of Nent.

naut, ON, 'cattle.' *Noutwath*. The corresponding OE nēat occurs in field-names.

nearu, OE, 'narrow place' or 'strait, difficulty.' Naworth Castle (?).

nigon, OE, 'nine.' Noonstones.

niþer, OE, 'nether.' Netherby, Netherhall.

nīwe, OE, 'new.' Newbiggin (4), Newby (2), Newlaithes, Newlands (5), Newsham, Newton, Newton Arlosh, Newton Reigny, Newtown (2), Westnewton. Also in field-names, where there are several more occurrences of 'new land(s).'

nook, modern English, occurs *passim* in field and minor names, but all the forms are late.

norþ, OE, 'north.' *Northmoor*, Normoss. Also in field-names.

norðmaðr, ON, 'northman (pretty certainly Norwegian).' Ormathwaite. The element may be a personal name.

ofer, OE, 'over, above.' Overby, Orthwaite.

oglen, Welsh, 'swamp.' (c) Desoglin (?).

onset, northern dialect, 'farmstead,' occurs several times in modern field and minor names. Cf. Grahams Onset and High Onset in Bewcastle and Simon's Onset in Nicholforest.

ōra, OE, 'ore.' Orgill. Cf. also *Orscarth*, a field-name in Birker.

orri, ON, 'blackcock,' possibly used as a personal name, could be the first element of Over Water, but the forms are much too late for any degree of certainty.

oxa, OE, 'ox.' Oxenriggs.

pæþ, OE, 'path,' occurs occasionally in minor or lost names, in the northern dialect form *peth*. Cf. Peth in Arthuret.

papi, ON, 'hermit.' Papcastle.

parke, ME from OFr, 'enclosure for beasts.' Park Ho, Fawepark, Isel Park.

pele, ME, 'a stake, palisade; a castle (especially a small castle or tower).' Peel Place. The word occurs also in other minor names for which there are only late forms, and in the early forms for Liddel Strength and High Head Castle.

pen(n), British, 'head,' also 'chief.' Penrith, Penruddock, Torpenhow.

penny, found in the field-names Penny Moss (Bewcastle), *Fourepeny Ferme* (Kingwater) and *Halfpenny Butts and Greaves* (Millom), may denote lands held by rents of that order, or be a term of contempt.

persone, ME from OFr, 'parson.' Parsonby.

perth, Welsh, 'thicket, brake.' The British equivalent of this is the second element of Solport (*c*), and a diminutive formed from the word is the source of Parton.

pete, ME, 'peat.' Peatmoor Wood, *Petegroves.* Occasionally in field-names.

pīc, OE, **pík,** ON, 'point, pointed mountain.' Red Pike, Stone Pike. Occasionally in field and other minor names.

piet, ME, 'magpie,' occurs occasionally in field and minor names. Cf. Pyetmire Wood in Hesket in the Forest and Pietnest in St John's. There is also a Pyeing Fm in Hesket, from ME *pie,* 'magpie,' and **eng.**

pigh(t)el, ME, 'small field, enclosure,' occurs occasionally in field-names, cf. *Pightelshead* in Hayton. The nasalised variant **pingel** and the modern form **pickle** both occur in field-names, **pingel** rather more frequently. **pickel** occurs in Pickle Bank.

place, ME, used in the sense 'manor-house.' Crakeplace Hall.

plasket occurs several times in field and minor names, the forms being modern. Cf. Plasket Plantation in Bromfield and Plasket-lands in Holme St Cuthbert. It may be an alternative form of the word *plashet* discussed PN Ess 489, derived from Late Latin *plassetum, plessetum* and meaning 'a fence of living wood.' Alternatively it may be a variant of the formally identical diminutive of *plash,* 'puddle.' Cf. PN W 443 (the forms *plashet* and *plaskett* are both found in W).

plūme, OE, 'plum, plum-tree.' Plumbland, Plumpton Wall.

plumpe, plompe, ME, 'clump.' Plump.

poll, ME, 'stream,' from a British word related to Welsh *pwll,* Cornish *poll.* (*a*) *Polgauer, Polneuton, Poltragon,* Poltross Burn, Pow Beck, *Powburgh, Pow Newton*; (*b*) Pow Maughan; (*c*) Wampool. Also in field-names. For a full discussion of the element *v.* RN 329–30. An extended form of this word may be contained in *Polterternan, Polterheued* and Powterneth Beck.

portcwēne, OE, 'prostitute.' Portinscale.

pot, ME, 'a deep hole.' *Ayntrepot,* Bishopspot, Black Pots, Thirlspot. Common in field-names.

prēost, OE, 'priest.' Preston, Priestcroft, Priestgill. Also in field-names.

prior, OE from Latin, 'prior.' Prior How, Prior Wood.

pundf(e)ald, OE, 'pinfold,' occurs in field-names.

pwll, Welsh, 'pool.' (*c*) Hellpool Bridge.

pyked, ME, 'pointed.' Picket How.

quarrel, a side-form of *quarry* which only survives in northern dialect, occurs several times in field and minor names. Cf. *La Quarelbryg* (1387, among early forms for Quarry Beck). It may be the first element of Wharrels Hill and Whorl Gill, with the substitution of [ʍ] for [kw] discussed *supra* xliii.

rá, ON, 'boundary, boundary mark.' Raby, Roe Beck.

rā, OE, 'roe-buck.' Rae Burn.

(v)rá, ON, 'nook, corner,' used of a secluded place. Wray Head, Wrayside, Wreah, Wreay (4), Aughtertree, Benwray, Bramery, Dockray (3), Lacra, Linedraw, Murrah, Rowrah (2), Scarrowhill, Sillerea Wood, Ullcat Row, Westray. Common in field-names.

rann, OIr, 'part, lot, share.' (*b*) Ravenglass.

ratoun, ME, **ratton**, modern northern dialect, 'rat.' Ratten Row (3), *Ratton rowe* (lost street-name in Carlisle). This compound also occurs four times as a field-name.

rauðr, ON, 'red.' Rockcliffe.

rāw, OE, 'row.' Baggara, Baggra Yeat, Baggrow, Baxter's Row, Bishop's Row, Ratten Row (3), *Ratton rowe* (a lost street-name in Carlisle). Common in field-names, where the name Ratten Row occurs several times.

rēad, OE, 'red.' Red Pike.

reik, ON, 'way, path,' is fairly common among field-names, and occurs in the modern form Rake in minor names for which only late forms are available, cf. *the Long Rake*, 1589 in Rockcliffe.

rein, ON, 'strip of land,' occurs frequently in field-names. Cf. *le Ranes*, 1423 in Dalston.

(v)reini, ON, 'stallion.' Wrynose.

rhiw, Welsh, 'slope, ascent.' The British equivalent of this is the second element of Cumrew.

rhynn, Welsh, 'headland.' The plural of a British word corresponding to this may be the source of Rinnion Hills.

ribbe, OE, 'rib-wort, hounds-tongue.' Ribton.

*ric, OE, 'stream.' Lostrigg Beck.

*risp, OE, 'brushwood.' *Respholm*. Also in field-names.

*riton, British, 'ford.' Penrith, Redmain.

riveling, an obsolete word of uncertain history meaning 'rivulet' (*v.* RN 343 for a discussion of its origin). Revelin Moss.

riving, perhaps connected with *outrive*, 'to break up (moor land or rough pasture land)' (NED), occurs in the field-names of Aspatria, Blencogo, Holm Cultram and Torpenhow. *Outrivings* occurs in Holm Cultram.

roche, ME, 'roach.' Roachburn.

ros, Irish, **rhos**, Welsh, 'moor.' The British word equivalent to these is the first element of *Raswraget* and probably the second element of Fletchers (*c*).

routande, ME, 'roaring.' Rentland Burn (?), Routenbeck. Several stream-names with this element occur among field-names.

rugr, ON, 'rye.' Ruckcroft.

rūh, OE, 'rough.' Rough Crag, Roughet Hill, Rougholme, Rowrah (2), Ruthwaite. Also in field-names.

runnr, ON, 'brake, thicket.' (*a*) Tymparon Hall; (*c*) *Poteruns*. Occasionally in field-names.

rysc, OE, 'rush.' The northern dialect *rash*, which is common in Cumberland field and minor names (cf. Rash and Wellrash in Boltons e.g.), is probably a variant of the OE *resce*, a form of the word recorded only once.

sǣ, OE, 'sea.' Seacote, Seascale, Seaton (?) (2), Silloth.

sætr, ON, 'summer-pasture farm, shieling.' (*a*) Seatoller, Baron Side, Blennerhasset, Greenside, Green Side, Kingside Hill, Lord's Seat, Racy Cott, Stubshead Hill, Swinside; (*b*) *Satgodard*, Setmabanning, Setmurthy, Annaside, *Arneshowe*, Fornside, Oughterside, *Randerside*, *Rogerside*. Fairly common in field-names.

s(e)alh, OE, 'willow.' Salkeld. Also in field-names and minor names for which only late forms are available.

s(e)alt, OE, 'salt.' Saltcoats, Salt Cotes, Salter, Salthouse. Cf. *Salt coote hylles* (1589), a field-name in Rockcliffe.

sand, OE, 'sand.' Sands, Sandale, Sandgate, Sandwith (2), Santon, Burgh by Sands. *Sandwath* occurs also as a field-name in Culgaith.

saurr, ON, 'mud, dirt.' Sosgill (2), Castle Sowerby, Sowerby Wood.

sauðr, ON, 'sheep,' may be the first element of Southwaite in Eaglesfield.

scad, NED sb², 'bullace' (*prunus insititia*) may be the first element of Scad Beck. If so it must have been in use much earlier than 1577, the date of the first recorded instance of it as an independent word in NED.

scamol, OE, 'stool, bench,' occurs occasionally in field and minor names, cf. *le Shambles*, 1619 in Penrith, *le Flesshameles*, 1348 in Carlisle.

*scawāco-, British, 'abounding in elders.' Chalk Beck.

sceaga, OE, 'small wood, copse, thicket.' Aikshaw, Brisco, Oakshaw. Also in field-names.

scearn, OE, 'dung,' occurs occasionally in field and minor names.

scēat, OE, 'point, or corner, of land.' Shatton (?). Also in field-names, cf. *Le Under Shott*, 1604 in Irthington.

scē(a)p, OE, 'sheep.' Skiprigg.

schele, ME, 'shepherd's summer hut, small house,' occurs in field and minor names, usually in the modern form Shield.

scinn, OE, 'demon.' Skinburness.

scīr, OE, 'district.' Skirwith.

scitere, a stream-name formed from an OE *scite*, 'dung.' A Scandinavianised form of this is the probable source of Bitter Beck and Skirting Beck.

scrogg, ME, 'a stunted bush, underwood,' occurs frequently in field and minor names. Catterlen Wood is *boscus de Caterlenscrok* in 1292.

scylf, OE, 'rock, pinnacle, crag; shelf, ledge.' Skelton.

sef, ON, 'sedge.' Seathwaite, Seavill (?). Also in field-names, where the adjective *Sevy-* is fairly common.

sel, ON, 'booth.' Brunshaw Moss.

sele, OE, 'hall, building.' Silecroft, *Speresele* (?).

selja, ON, 'willow.' Selker, Sillerea Wood.

seofon, OE, 'seven.' Sewborwens, Hallsenna.

seolfor, OE, 'silver.' Silver Beck, Silver Side.

sīc, OE, 'small stream.' (*a*) Sikeside, Aigill Sike, Black Sike, Eel Sike, Foulsyke, Withe Sike; (*c*) Wallmoorsike. Occurs frequently in field-names, and minor names for which there are only late forms.

sīde, OE, 'side; slope of a hill, bank.' *Byrkensydvanell*, Edderside, Fawcettlees, Silver Side, Stonegarthside, Woodside. Also in field-names.

sík, ON, equivalent to **sīc** *supra*. Hazel Sike, Kelsick, *Kerlingsik*.

sine, a northern dialect verb meaning 'to drain,' probably occurs in Siney Tarn and Sinen Gill.

sión, ON, 'view.' Shundraw (?).

skáli, ON, cognate with **schele** *supra*, and used in the same sense. (*a*) Scale, Scales (4), Low Scales, Scaleby, Scalefield Gill Plantation, Scale Gill, Scalegill Hall, Scalehouses, Scalelands, Scalescough, Scarrowhill, Skelgill (2), Skelling, *Scoggarbar*, Borrowscale (2), Bowscale (2), Deanscale, Foxley Henning, Gatesgill, Howscales, Linskeldfield, Portinscale, Seascale, Sosgill (2), Stubsgill, Winscales (2), Winskill, Winter Shields; (*b*) Scarrowmanwick, *Skalmallock*, Gutherscale, Keskadale, *Ketelscalerbech*, Rogerscale, Simonscales. Frequent in field-names.

skalli, ON, 'bald head,' used as a nickname for a hill, is probably contained in Sca Fell, Scallow, High Scawdel and several field-names.

skarð, ON, 'notch, cleft, mountain pass.' Scar Gill, Scargreen, Scawbank, Starthill, Gatesgarth (2), *Troscart*, *Wainscarth*. Also in field-names.

skeið, ON, 'race-course.' *Brunskaith*, Brunstock, Hesket in the Forest.

sker, ON, 'rock, reef.' (*a*) Scare; (*b*) Barn Scar. Also in field-names

skiallr, ON, 'resounding.' Skill Beck (?).

skit, ON, 'filth.' Skitwath Beck.

skjǫldr, ON, 'shield.' Skelda.

skógr, ON, 'wood,' cognate with **sceaga.** (*a*) Scaws, Sceugh, Sceugh Hill Wood, Schoose, Aldersceugh, Brisco(e), Ellershaw Plantation, Flaska, Fluskew, *Gilderskugh*, Haresceugh, Lambsceugh, Lofshaw Hill, Losca (?), Middlesceugh, Morton Sceugh, Northsceugh, Scalescough; (*b*) Huddlesceugh, Rogersceugh, Scalderscew. Fairly frequent in early field-names.

skot, ON, 'projecting piece of land, rising hill,' sometimes 'place where timber is shot down a hill.' Scoat Fell.

Skoti, ON, 'Scot.' Scotby.

skreið, ON, 'landslide.' *Scraithegill.*

skúti, ON, 'overhanging rock.' Skiddaw (?).

slæp, OE, 'slippery place,' occurs occasionally in field and minor names, three times in combination with stān—Slapestone, Slapestones, and *Sleape Stone* (1660 in Eskdale fields).

slāh, OE, 'sloe.' Sleathwaite. The Scandinavian cognate of this, which appears as *slaaen* in ODan, *slān* OSw, occurs in South Slealands.

slakki, ON, 'shallow valley.' Castle Slack. Also in field-names and in minor names for which there are only late forms.

slétta, ON, 'plain, level field.' Sleet Beck (?), Sleightholme.

smá(r), ON, 'small.' Smaithwaite (2).

smeoru, OE, **smjǫr,** ON, 'fat, grease,' used in place-names to describe good grazing ground, occurs occasionally in field-names. Cf. Smearburgh in Dalston.

snab, northern dialect word used for 'a steep place or ascent; a rugged rise or point,' occurs several times in field and minor names, cf. Snab End in Alston, Snab in Caldbeck, Snab Murris in Dean and High and Low Snab in Above Derwent. The origin of the word is uncertain, but NED compares Middle Flemish *snabbe*, apparently used of a point of land, and later Flemish *snabbe, snab,* 'beak.' The forms from 1503 for High and Low Snab and 1684 for Snab Murris show the word to have been in use considerably earlier than 1797, the date of the first example in NED.

snāw, OE, 'snow.' Snowden Close.

snittle, dialect word of obscure origin meaning 'noose, snare.' Snittlegarth (?).

sol, OE, 'muddy place.' Solway Moss.

*spearca or ***spearce,** OE, 'brushwood.' Sparket.

spell, OE, 'speech.' The Spillers (?).

spere, OE, 'spear.' *Speresele* (?).

spitel, ME from OFr *hospital,* 'hospital.' Spital, *Spittlesdike.*

spoute, ME, occurs in the following field and minor names: *Spute-kelde* (c. 1200 in Farlam, c. 1250 in Lamplugh), *Spute* (c. 1300 in Broughton), Spout Meadow (in Corney, Waberthwaite and Whicham), Spout Field (in Upper Denton), Spout Close (in Dean) and Spout Ho (in Loweswater). The word is first recorded in NED in 1392, and in the earliest references there it is used of a pipe through which water flows and is discharged. The modern northern dialect meanings recorded in EDD (*spout* vb and sb 10 and 11), 'a small waterfall; a stream of no great volume of water' and 'a boggy spring in the ground,' are more appropriate to these field-names, especially the early compound *Sputekelde*.

spring, ME, 'copse of young trees.' Hazelspring. The word also occurs as a field-name (1568) in Ainstable.

stafn, ON, 'stock, pole.' Stephney.

stafr, ON, 'post, pole.' Staffield.

stakkr, ON, possibly in the sense 'pillar of rock.' Stockdale (?).

stān, OE, 'stone.' (*a*) Stainburn, Stainton (3), Stone Beck, Stone-garthside, Stone Ho, *Caldewstones*, Dry Stone Knott, Greason Cottage, Greystones, Noonstones, Standing Stones; (*b*) Brownel-son; (*c*) Sprunston. Very frequent in field-names. Standing Stones occurs several times as a minor name with late forms. *v.* also **græg** *supra* and **tūn** *infra*.

stand, ME, 'hunter's stand for shooting game.' High Stand.

stānig, OE, 'stony.' Stony How.

stank, 'a pond or pool,' now only surviving in Scotland and in English dialect, occurs several times in field and minor names. Cf. Stankend in Holme Abbey.

stapol, OE, 'pillar.' Stapleton.

staðir, ON, plural of **staðr**, which is cognate with **stede** *infra*, and means 'place, town.' (*b*) Honister Crag (?).

stede, OE, 'place, position, site.' (*a*) Byerstead, Castlesteads (2), Hallsteads (2); (*b*) Dormansteads. Fairly common in field-names, where the first element is often a word for a building. There are five 'house-steads' (in Brampton, Upper Denton, Egremont, Irthing-ton and Plumbland), a 'barn-stead' (Penrith) and other examples of 'byre-stead' (Crosscanonby) and 'hall-stead' (Setmurthy). Modern *stead* occurs in field and minor names with a Christian or surname prefixed, but less frequently than *town* (*v. infra* **tūn**). The element is often in the plural.

steinn, ON, 'stone,' cognate with **stān** *supra*. (*a*) Stanwix, Stone How, Stone Pike, Stonethwaite, Braystones, Brig Stones; (*b*) *Stan-brennan, Staynlenok*.

stīg, OE, **stíg**, ON, 'path.' (*a*) Bransty, Wolsty, Sty Head; (*b*) Starling Dodd (?). Also in field-names.

stigel, OE, 'stile.' Steel End. Frequent in field-names.

stoc, OE, 'place.' (*a*) Linstock; (*c*) Greystoke (?).

stocc, OE, 'stock, trunk of a tree.' (*a*) Stockbridge, Stockley Bridge; (*c*) Greystoke (?). Also in field-names.

stōd, OE, 'stud, herd of horses.' Stoddah, Studholme. **stōdf(e)ald**, OE, 'stud enclosure,' occurs in field-names.

stokk, ON, equivalent to **stocc** *supra*. Stockdalewath.

stǫng, ON (stang- in compounds), 'pole, stake.' Stanger, Stangrah, Stangs Bridge.

stǫrr, ON (star- in compounds), 'sedge.' Stare Beck, Stargill, Starnmire. Also in field-names.

storð, ON, 'brushwood.' Storth Brow. Also in field-names.

stott, OE, 'horse, bullock.' Stotgill.

strand, OE, 'shore, bank.' Strands (2). Occasionally in field-names.

strete, ME, modern **street**, occurs rather late as the second element of street-names in Carlisle.

strōd, OE, 'marshy land overgrown with brushwood.' Long Strath, Strudda Bank.

stubb, OE, 'tree-stump.' *Stubhill*, Stubsgill, Stubshead Hill. There is another *Stubhill* in the field-names of Wigton.

súl, ON, 'pillar.' Solway Firth.

sundor-, OE, 'separate, remote; private, special.' Sunderland.

*sunt, OE, 'swamp.' *Sunton* (?).

sūtere, OE, 'cobbler.' Souther Fell, Southerfield.

suðrœnn, ON, 'southern.' Southernby.

svali, ON, 'swallow.' Swabies. The element may be a personal name.

svart-r, ON, 'dark.' Swarthgill, *Swarthow*.

sviðinn, ON, 'land cleared by burning.' *Swithenthate.*

swang, northern dialect word meaning 'swamp,' occurs several times in field-names, cf. *the low Swange*, 1716 in Hesket in the Forest.

swealwe, OE, 'swallow.' Swallowhurst.

swēora, OE, 'neck, col,' is probably the first element of Swire Sike, though no early forms have been found.

*Swifte, an OE river-name from *swift*, 'rapid' (*v.* RN 387). The Swifts.

swīn, OE, 'pig.' Swinside (2).

tal, Welsh, 'brow, end.' A British equivalent occurs in Tallentire, Talkin.

tenter, from ME *teyntur*, 'a wooden framework on which cloth is stretched after being milled, so that it may set or dry evenly and without shrinking,' occurs about eight times in field and minor names; cf. Tenterbank Wood in Brampton.

terrig, Welsh, 'ardent, severe.' A British word corresponding to this is contained in Tory Bridge.

þak, ON, 'thatch,' used in place-names to denote a place where reeds for thatching grow. Thackmire, Thack Moor, Thakthwaite (3). Fairly frequent in field-names.

þeof, OE, 'thief.' Thethwaite, Thiefside Hill.

þing, OE and ON, 'assembly.' Fingland (?).

þistel, OE, **þistill**, ON, 'thistle.' Thistleton, Thistlewood.

þōh, OE, 'clay.' Southwaite (in Hesket).

þorn, OE and ON, 'thorn-bush.' Thornbank, Thornbarrow, Thorn Hill, Thornholme, Thornthwaite Beck, Thornthwaite (3), Townhead, Anthorn, Bowthorn, Court Thorn. Also in field-names.

þorp, ON, **þrop**, OE, 'farm, hamlet.' (a) Thorpe, Throp; (c) Cracrop.

þræll, ON, 'thrall.' Threlkeld.

þrangr, ON, 'compressed.' Thrangholm.

þrēap-, OE, stem of the verb *þrēapian*, 'to contend, dispute.' Debateable Land (alternatively *Threpelandez*), Threapland, Threapthwaite. There are three more occurrences in field-names, *Threipheing*, c. 1245 in Gilcrux, *Threaptongue*, 1587 in Eskdale, and Threapland Gate in Drigg.

þveit, ON, 'piece cut out or off' hence 'parcel of land, clearing, paddock.' (a) Thwaites (2), Applethwaite, Arrowthwaite (3), Binthwaite Plantation, *Blaburthwaite*, Blaithwaite, Brackenthwaite (3), Braithwaite (2), Branthwaite (2), Bruthwaite, Burnthwaite, Burthwaite Bridge, Calthwaite, Cringlethwaite Terrace, Crosthwaite, Curthwaite, Curthwaite Beck, Easthwaite, Foggythwaite, Haithwaite, Haythwaite Lane, Hewthwaite, *Hothwaite*, Lanthwaite Green, *Langthwaite*, Langthwaite, Legburthwaite, Linethwaite, Longthwaite (4), Lothwaite (?), Micklethwaite, Moorthwaite (2), Mossthwaite, Murthwaite Moor, Orthwaite, Outhwaite, Reathwaite, Roughethill, Ruthwaite, Seathwaite, Shoulthwaite, Smaithwaite (2), Southwaite, Stonethwaite, *Swithenthate*, Thackthwaite (3), Thethwaite, Thistlewood, Thornthwaite (3), Thornthwaite Beck, Townthwaite Beck, Threapthwaite, Waberthwaite, Wallthwaite, Wanthwaite, Wythwaite; (b) *Thueitdounegaleg*', Austhwaite, Bassenthwaite, Dowthwaitehead, Godderthwaite, Scawthwaite Close, Wickerthwaite; (c) Mousthwaite Comb, Ormathwaite, *Postlethwaite*. Occurs *passim* in field-names.

þyrel, OE, 'hollow,' might be the first element of Thirlmere.

þyrnir, ON, 'thorn-bush.' *Thirneby* (?).

þyrs, OE, **þurs**, ON, 'giant.' Thirlspot, *Thruswell*. There are three occurrences in field-names, *Thursgill*' (1384 Hesket in the Forest), *Thyrspoone* (1568 Ainstable) and *Thrushhowe* (1578 Nether Wasdale).

*tī-, tei-, Celtic, 'to dissolve, to flow.' South Tyne, *Tyne Sike* (?).

timbr, ON, 'timber.' Birchtimber Hill.

tiompan, Irish, 'small abrupt hill, standing stone.' Tymparon Hall.

tiǫrn, ON, 'tarn.' (*a*) Tarns, Tarn Beck, Blea Tarn, Bleatarn, Blind Tarn (2), Dock Tarn, *Goseterne*, Talkin Tarn, Tindale Tarn; (*b*) *Tarn Marron*, Tarn Wadling, Martin Tarn; (*c*) Floutern Tarn, Sprinkling Tarn. Also in field-names.

tir, Welsh, 'land.' A corresponding British word occurs in Tallentire.

todhole, ME, 'fox-earth.' Toddell, Todholes, Toddhills Wood. There are numerous occurrences of **tod** and **todhole** in field-names and other minor names for which the forms are late.

tor, British, 'peak, hill.' Tercrosset, Torkin, Torpenhow.

tōte, ME, 'look-out hill,' occurs several times in field and minor names, but the forms are late. Cf. Tute Hill in Cockermouth, Tottle Hill in Kirkland and Blencarn, Toothill in Caldbeck.

*traneberi, ME, corresponding to Sw *tranbär*, Dan *tranebær*, 'cranberry.' Cranberry Moss.

trani, ON, 'crane.' Stranmoss Wood. There are two occurrences in field-names of this compound with **mos** (Cumwhitton and Ainstable), and two of **trani** and **mýrr** (Hayton and Wetheral). Cf. also *Le Crayne myer close*, 1609 in St Cuthbert Without.

tré, ON, 'tree.' *Ayntrepot*. The corresponding OE **trēo(w)** occurs occasionally in field-names.

treb, OWelsh, 'homestead.' The British equivalent occurs in Blennerhasset, Triermain.

trod, a dialect word meaning 'path, trackway,' from ON *troð*, occurs occasionally in field-names: cf. *Church Trodds*, 1722 in Hesket in the Forest.

trog, OE, 'trough, valley.' Trough, Troughfoot.

tros, ON, 'brushwood.' *Troscart*.

truht, OE, 'trout.' Trout Beck (3), Troutbeck, *troutbecke*. There is another *Trutebek'* (1292) among the field-names of Greystoke, and a modern one in the field-names of Kirkoswald.

*trun, *turn, OE, 'circular place.' Turnberry Ho.

tūn, OE, 'enclosed piece of ground, homestead, village.' (*a*) Townend, Town End, Aikton, Angerton (2), Brampton, Brayton, Broughton, Clifton, Coulderton, Crofton, Denton, Easton (2), Ellerton, Fenton, Hayton (2), Haytongate, Houghton, Hutton, Hyton, Irthington, Irton, Itonfield, Kelton, Kirkbampton, Kirklinton, Lanerton, Longtown, Milton, Morton (2), Morton Sceugh, Newton, Newton Arlosh, Newton Reigny, Westnewton, Newtown (2), Plumpton Wall, Preston, Randalinton, Raughton, Ribton, Santon, Seaton (2), Shatton, Skelton, Stainton (3), Stapleton,

Thistleton, Upton, Walton (2), Waverton, Welton, Westlinton, Wilton; (b) Alston, Askerton, Dalston, Embleton, Orton, Oulton, Wigton; (c) Camerton, Lorton, *Satherton*.

The element is rare in field-names, but there is another *Eston*' (1292 in Arthuret) and three more names in which the first element is either OE stān or ON steinn (*Stanton* 1294 in Haile, *Staynton* 1250–93 in Millom and *Steynton*' 1285 in Wigton). Modern *town* occurs in a considerable number of minor names, mostly in Eskdale and Cumberland Wards, with a Christian name or surname prefixed. The forms for these names are late. Cf. Antonstown, Nixonstown and Scotstown in Bewcastle.

tunge, OE, **tunga,** ON, 'tongue,' used in place-names of a tongue of land. Tongue (2), Tongue Head, Tongue Moor, Middle Tongue, Townthwaite Beck, Bleng Tongue.

tví-, ON, 'two.' *Thuahovel*.

ufera, OE, 'over.' Overby, Orthwaite.

ūle, OE, 'owl.' Ulcat Row, Ullcoats. ON **ugla** may be the first element of Uglygill.

úlfr, ON, 'wolf.' Uldale (?), Uldale Fm, Ullock (2), Ulpha.

unþanc, OE, 'ill-will, displeasure.' Unthank (3).

uppe, OE, 'up, above.' Upton.

ūtgang, OE, 'way out,' later used of 'a road by which cattle go out to pasture.' Outgang Wood. Occurs about half-a-dozen times in field-names.

vangr, ON, or **wang,** OE, 'meadow.' Whangs.

vargr, ON, 'wolf; outlaw.' Wragmire (?).

varði, ON, 'cairn, heap of stones.' (a) Ward Hall; (b) *Watchcomon*.

vað, ON, 'ford.' (a) Wath (2), Bleawath, Botlands Blawith, Broadwath, Crookwath, Dubwath, *Dub Wath*, Lairthwaite, Langwathby, Linewath, *Monkwath*, *Noutwath*, Sandwith (2), Skitwath Beck, Solway Firth, Stockdalewath; (b) Kersey Bridge, *Thoroldwath*, *Waspatrickwath*; (c) Brocklewath, Southwaite. Fairly common in field-names.

vatn, ON, 'water, lake.' Wasdale, Wast Water, Watendlath.

veggr, ON, 'wall.' Stanwix.

veiðr, ON, 'hunting, fishing.' Waburthwaite, Wedholme Flow.

vennel, ME, from OFr, 'a narrow lane or passage in a town or city,' used in Scotland and the north of England, occurs a number of times in field-names and lost street-names. Cf. *Blind-Venell* (1621), *Byrkensydvanell* (1498), *St Mungo venall* (1662) and *Shap Vennell* (1597), all in Carlisle.

vík, ON, 'bay.' Fleswick Bay.

vin, ON, 'meadow, grazing place.' Rosewain.

viðr, ON, 'wood.' Skirwith.

wæfre, OE, 'wandering.' Waver.

*wærna, OE, a metathesised derivative of **wrænna*, genitive plural of **wræna*, 'stallion.' Warnell (?).

wæter, OE, 'water.' (*a*) Waterend, Crummock Water, Derwent Water, Devoke Water, Ennerdale Water, Loweswater, Wast Water; (*b*) Ullswater. It is the second element of the earliest forms for Bassenthwaite Lake.

wain, ME, 'waggon.' *Wainscarth*.

w(e)ald, OE, 'forest land,' later 'open country.' Wodow Bank, *Cnokdentwald*.

walke, ME, 'to full (cloth).' Wallthwaite (?). Walk-mill, 'fulling mill,' occurs in the field-names of several parishes.

w(e)all, OE, 'wall.' Walby, Walton (2); see also p. xvii *supra*.

wandale occurs four times in the county, in Skelton, Skirwith, Thursby and Wetheral, the forms being 16th century or later. It is an obsolete dialect word denoting a share of the open arable land of a township. It has been noted, with much earlier forms, in a number of counties, the general distribution suggesting Scandinavian origin. In PN ERY 107 it is suggested that it contains OScand *vǫndr*, 'twig,' and *deill*, 'share of land,' the meaning apparently being either a piece of land marked off with stakes or one measured off with a wand.

w(e)ard, OE, 'stronghold.' Naworth Castle. *warde*, ME, used of an administrative division, here a division of a forest, is the second element of Westward. See Introduction, pp xiv–xv.

waroð, OE, 'bank, shore.' Warwick.

welig, wylig, OE, 'willow.' *Will Ave* (?), Wilton. Also in field-names and minor names for which the forms are late.

w(i)elle, OE, 'spring, stream.' Welton, *Carswelhowe*, Greenwell, Seaville.

went, a ME word meaning 'path, passage,' obsolete except in dialect, occurs several times in field-names and lost street-names. Cf. *Wenthead*, 1743 in Whitehaven.

wēod, OE, 'weed.' Weddicar.

wernægel, OE, 'tumour on the back of cattle,' possibly used as a hill-name. Warnell (?).

west, OE, 'west.' Wescoe, West End, Westfield Ho, Westgarth, Westgarth-hill, Westlinton, The West March, Westray, Westward. Also in field-names.

weþer, OE, '(castrated) ram.' Watermillock, Wetheral, Wetheriggs.

whin, ME, 'gorse, whin,' probably of Scandinavian origin. Whin-bank, Whinbarrow Ho, Whinfell, Whin Fell, Whinlatter, Whinny-hill, Winnow. Also in field-names.

wīc, OE, 'village, dairy farm.' (*a*) Keswick, Warwick; (*b*) Renwick.

wind, OE, 'wind.' Winder (2), Winscales (2), Winskill.

windgeat, OE, 'pass through which the wind sweeps.' Wind Gap.

winter, OE, 'winter.' Winter Shields.

wiðig, OE, 'willow.' Whit Beck (2) (?), Withe Sike, Wythburn, *Wytheskeld*, Wythop, Wythwaite. Also in field-names.

wudu, OE, 'wood.' (*a*) Wood End, Woodend (3), Wood Hall, Woodhall (2), *Woodhouse*, Woodside, Baronwood, Blackhall Wood, Boltonwood, Bridgewood Foot, *Foulwood*, Gelt Woods, Inglewood Forest, Orton Wood, Skelton Wood End, Sowerby Wood, Talkinhead Wood, Walton Wood; (*c*) Wanwood Ho. Also in field-names. Woodside and Woodhouse(s) are common among modern minor names.

wulf, OE, 'wolf.' Wolsty (?), Wooloaks.

wyrm, OE, 'reptile, snake.' Worm Gill, Woundell Beck.

yad, north country form of *jade*, 'a work-horse or mare; an old, worn-out horse,' occurs several times in field and minor names. Cf. Hadyaud Sike, Hodyoad in Lamplugh, *Yawdfalld* (1603 in Kirkandrews) and *Yad Closes* (1649 in Holme Cultram).

yoking, a term for a measure of land, occurs several times in field-names. Cf. Busy, Long and Stoney Yokeing in Bewcastle. *v*. NED for the exact proportions of the strip.

ysbyddaden, Welsh, 'hawthorn.' Spadeadam (?).

NOTES ON THE DISTRIBUTION
OF THESE ELEMENTS

The British elements in the place-names of the county are not discussed here. For a detailed analysis of their distribution and significance, *v*. Introduction, pp. xvii–xx.

The references to other counties are based on the material in PN NRY, Ekwall's *Place-Names of Lancashire* and Mawer's *Place-Names of Northumberland and Durham*. It should be remembered that those surveys are less detailed than the present one of Cumberland, particularly as regards field and minor names, and comparison of the frequency and distribution of elements in the various counties cannot be very precise.

bekkr is much the most common stream-name element among names which have survived, but in early field-names this word and OE sīc or ON sík are equally frequent. The element is common in NRY and fairly frequent in La, but it has not been noted in early names in Nb and Du.

be(o)rg and hyll are about as common as each other, although it is difficult to be certain about the frequency or distribution of the former because it is often impossible to distinguish it from ON berg. Of the fourteen names which have been assumed to contain be(o)rg, six are in Allerdale above, two in Allerdale below Derwent, and there are four in Leath and one in Cumberland and Eskdale Wards. Of the twelve names given in the list of elements as containing hyll, five are in Cumberland Ward, four in Leath and three in Eskdale. It thus appears that hyll is rather more usual in the north and east of the county and be(o)rg in the west and south, and this impression is confirmed by an examination of the early field-name material. be(o)rg is the more common of the two elements in NRY, but hyll is the only one recorded in Nb and Du. hyll is rare in La north of the Ribble.

berg. Of ten names given in the list of elements as containing this word, five are in Allerdale above Derwent, one in Allerdale below and four in Leath Wards.

bōþ: v. búð *infra*.

bōðl, bōtl (the characteristic northern forms of the OE word which also appears as *bold* elsewhere) is found three times, all in the west of the county. The two occurrences of bōðltūn are also in the west. In NRY, La and Nb and Du the word similarly occurs but is rare.

brōc occurs only in Broughton and in two field-names, *Suuinebrokeil* (1200) in Castle Carrock and *Nereherebrokes* (c. 1210) in Westlinton. The word is fairly common in La (Broughton occurs three times in Lancashire North-of-the-Sands), but is not recorded as an early element in Nb and Du and is rare in NRY.

burghan. The occurrences of this element, including those in field-names, are noticeably concentrated in the south and east of the county—there are eleven in Leath, ten in Allerdale above Derwent, four in Allerdale below Derwent and four in Cumberland Wards.

burh and burhstede occur, the former about a dozen times including early field-names and the latter only once, but no instance of burhtūn has been noted. burh is not compounded with a personal name, and in two instances it refers to a Roman fort. It is rather more common than cæster, which in three instances refers to a Roman fort and is twice compounded with a personal name. castel is once (Maiden-castle) applied to an ancient earthwork and twice (Castlesteads in Walton and Plumpton Wall) to a Roman fort: in most of the examples it probably refers to a medieval castle. In NRY burh is fairly frequent and cæster not found at all. burh is about as common in Nb and Du as in Cu, and rather more common in La: ceaster occurs in these counties.

burna is more frequent than **brōc**. With the exception of Stainburn in the extreme west, all the examples are in the east of the county near the borders of Nb and Du in which counties **burna** is the regular word for a small stream. There are several examples in Alston, which belongs physiographically to Nb and Du. It is fairly common in La and NRY.

búð. To the four examples given in the list of elements should be added two field-names, *Levedibuthes* (c. 1210) in Tallentire and *Marcebuthe* (1209–10) in Borrowdale. Five of the examples are in Allerdale above and one in Allerdale below Derwent. The three examples of ODan **bōþ** (Armboth, Boat How and *Crumwelbothye*, a. 1292 in Corney) are in these Wards. There are several examples of **búð** in north La (three north of the Sands), but none in NRY or in Nb and Du. **bōþ** is more common in La than it is in Cu, but not in the north.

bȳ is very frequent, and is distributed evenly over the county. The first element is a personal name, which may be Scandinavian, English, Celtic or Continental, in more than half of the occurrences. The word is much less common in Du (it does not occur in Nb) and in La than it is in Cu, but considerably more frequent in NRY. In Cu it was certainly still in use as a formative suffix in the 12th century, *v.* Introduction, pp. xxxi–xxxiii.

bygging occurs about eight times, including field-names, the compound Newbiggin being repeated four times. There is one example with a personal name. The word is about equally common in NRY (where there are five examples with 'new') and in Nb and Du (where Newbiggin occurs twice). There are two examples of Newbigging in La.

cot(e) occurs ten times (once in the field-name *Morcote* in Haile). It is not compounded with a personal name. The element is rather more common in NRY and La, and rather less common in Nb and Du.

dæl is difficult to distinguish from **dalr**, but is fairly certain to occur in the eleven names given against it in the list of elements. It is more frequent than **denu**, of which there are three certain and one possible examples. **denu** is very common in Nb and Du, where **dæl**, **dalr** are rather rare, but rare in NRY and La North-of-the-Sands, where **dæl**, **dalr** are frequent. Most of the examples of **dæl** are in Eskdale and Cumberland Wards, while of the names containing **denu**, Arlecdon, Dean and Duddon are in Allerdale above Derwent, and Denton in Eskdale Wards. With two exceptions, the thirty names given in the list of elements under **dalr** are in Allerdale above Derwent, Allerdale below Derwent and Leath Wards, most of them in the two former.

dūn is very rare. It is common in Nb and Du, but rather rare in La (there are no examples in La North-of-the-Sands) and NRY.

(ī)eg is very rare, in marked contrast to **holmr**. **hamm** does not occur in the county. **(ī)eg** is rare in NRY, where **holmr** is similarly very frequent and **hamm** not recorded. All three words are rare in Nb and Du. **(ī)eg** is more common in La than in Cu, **holmr** very frequent, and **hamm** probably does not occur.

eng. The occurrences of this word in early field-names are mostly in Allerdale above and below Derwent Wards.

erg. The names containing this element are concentrated in Allerdale above Derwent and Leath Wards, *v.* Introduction, p. xxiv. The word is not recorded in Nb and Du, is not so frequent in NRY as in Cu, and is more frequent in La.

feld is common, and is twice compounded with a personal name. It is fairly frequent in Nb and Du and in La, but rare in NRY.

fell is common. It is not recorded in Nb and Du, rare in NRY, and less common in La than in Cu.

fenn and **mersc** occur only once, the latter in the field-name *Merscland*, a. 1240 in Burgh by Sands. **mōr** and **mýrr** are common, the latter especially as a field-name element. **fenn** is rather more frequent in Nb and Du than in Cu, but not recorded at all in La or NRY. **mersc** is less rare in these four counties than it is in Cu.

fit. Of the names given in the list of elements, four are in Allerdale above and one in Allerdale below Derwent. The early field-names which contain the element are mostly in these two Wards.

garðr is very common and evenly distributed over the county. It occurs once in Du (not at all in Nb), but is fairly common in La and NRY.

gata is the most common word for a street or way. OE *weg* does not occur in the county. In some late street-name forms *gate* alternates with *street*. **gata** is common in NRY and occurs in a few major names in Nb and Du and in La. There is one example of *weg* in Du and one in NRY. It is not recorded in major names in La.

gil is very common and is several times compounded with a personal name. The original sense of the word is 'ravine,' but in Cumberland it is one of the most frequent elements in stream-names. It is fairly common in NRY, but less frequent in La and not recorded in Nb and Du.

h(e)alh. The nominative form, much less common in place-names than the oblique form, appears in Ameshaugh and *Kirkhalgh* (c. 1340–50) in Dalston. The element is not common in Cu or NRY, but is much more frequent in Nb and Du and La.

hām is rather rare (ten examples) in contrast to **tūn**. The element is only slightly more common in NRY than in Cu, somewhat more frequent in La and very much more common in Nb and Du.

haugr is very common, and is about ten times compounded with a personal name. It is definitely more frequent in Leath and Allerdale above and below Derwent Wards than in Eskdale and Cumberland. The element is about equally common in NRY, rather less common in La and not recorded at all in Nb and Du.

hlāw is rather rare and is never compounded with a personal name. **hōh** is more frequent. **hlāw** is very common in Nb and Du, fairly common in La, but not recorded at all in NRY. **hōh** is about equally frequent in Cu, NRY and La, but more common in Nb and Du.

holmr is very frequent, and distributed evenly over the county. It is occasionally compounded with a personal name. It is rare in Nb and Du but common in NRY and La.

hop, a distinctively Anglian element, occurs but is not frequent. There are ten examples including those in field-names. The word is very common in Nb and Du, about as frequent in La as in Cu, and less frequent in NRY.

hrycg and **hryggr** are very frequent, considerably more so than in NRY, Nb and Du or La.

hyll. *v.* b(e)org *supra.*

-ing and **-ingas** do not occur in the county. For the distribution of names in **-ingahām** and **-ing(a)tūn**, *v.* Introduction, p. xxi.

kelda is common both as a first and second element, and occurs quite frequently with a personal name. It is common in NRY but occasional in La and Nb and Du.

land is fairly common in names which have survived and very common in early field-names, where it often occurs in the plural. In Gilsland the first element is a personal name. The word is less common in major names in NRY and Nb and Du and about equally frequent in La.

lē(a)h occurs but is not very common. It is very frequent indeed in La (though very few examples are north of the Sands) and in Nb and Du; and in NRY, where it is much less common than in these three counties, there are still nearly four times as many examples as in Cu.

lundr occurs but is not common. It is rare in La also and not recorded in Nb and Du, but fairly common in NRY.

(v)rá is common, and is used by itself and as a second element. It is another of the ON elements which are noticeably more common in Allerdale above and below Derwent and Leath than in the other two Wards. It occurs in NRY but only as a field-name element, and is less common in La than in Cu, though most of the La examples are in the north of the county. It is not recorded in Nb and Du.

sætr is common, and is much more frequent in Allerdale above and below Derwent and in Leath than in the other two Wards. It occurs about ten times in combination with a personal name. It is perhaps a little more common in Cu than in Nb and Du, La and NRY, but it is difficult to be certain without a survey of the field-names of the latter counties.

sceaga is rather rare, and the cognate ON skógr rather frequent. skógr is more frequent in Cu than in La or NRY; it is not recorded in Nb and Du. In La there are two examples of skógr north of the Sands, and none of sceaga, though the latter is rather common in the rest of the county.

sīc and the corresponding ON sík are fairly frequent, especially in early field-names. They are fairly frequent in NRY but rare in La and apparently not found at all in Nb and Du.

skáli is very common. It occurs by itself and as a first and second element, and about eight times with a personal name. It is much more common in Cu than in La (where, however, a fair proportion of the examples are north of the Sands) or NRY, and is apparently not found at all in Nb and Du, where ME schele is common.

stede. To the five names given in the list of elements can be added about eight occurrences in 13th century field-names and a considerable number of examples of modern *stead* in field and minor names. The element is apparently rare in La, Nb and Du and NRY.

stoc is very rare. No examples have been noted in field-names to be added to the two in the list of elements, and the word is equally rare in surrounding counties. In those being used for comparison, it is only recorded in La, where there are three examples.

þorp and þrop are rare. No occurrences have been noted in field-names. þorp is common in NRY, but is rare in La and in Nb and Du.

þveit is very common indeed, more so in Allerdale above and below Derwent and Leath than in the other two Wards. It occurs most often as a second element, but occasionally by itself or as the first element of an inversion compound, and there are about seven examples in which it occurs with a personal name. The element is common in La and NRY, but not found at all in Nb and Du.

tiọrn is the commonest word for a lake, more frequent than OE wæter or ON vatn, which refer to larger pieces of water.

tūn is common, and fairly evenly distributed over the county. The element is very common in La, NRY and Nb and Du.

-um. The dative plural ending is not common. It occurs in Glaramara, *Hougenai*, Millom, Newsham, *Solom Moss* and possibly *Horrum*, a field-name in Millom. Three of these names are in the parish of Millom.

vað is rather common, much more so than ford. It occurs most frequently as a second element but occasionally by itself. There are three examples with a personal name. Of the elements vað and ford, the former is more frequent in NRY and the latter in La. vað does not occur in Nb and Du, where ford is very common.

w(e)ald occurs, but is rare. It is not recorded in La or Nb and Du, but there are five examples in NRY.

w(i)elle is rare. It is more common in NRY, La and Nb and Du than in Cu, though there is only one example in La North-of-the-Sands.

wīc is rare. There is one example with a personal name. It is rare in NRY, somewhat more frequent in La and much more frequent in Nb and Du.

worþ does not occur in the county. It is fairly common in Nb and Du and La, but occurs only once in NRY.

wudu is fairly common and evenly distributed over the county. The cognate ON viðr occurs only once. wudu is about equally common in Nb and Du and in La as in Cu, but less frequent in NRY. viðr is more common in NRY.

PERSONAL NAMES COMPOUNDED IN CUMBERLAND PLACE-NAMES

Names not found in independent use are marked with a single asterisk if they can be inferred from evidence other than that of the place-name in question. Such names may be regarded as hardly less certain than those which have no asterisk. The date and the parish are given where the place-name in which the personal name occurs is a field-name.

(a) OLD ENGLISH

Adda (Addingham), *Æðelsige* (*Elsycrok*, *Helsycroft*, 1303 in Ellenborough, *Elseycroft*, 1578 in Muncaster), *Æðelweard* (Allerby), *Aldgȳð* (f) (Bewaldeth, *Alditcroft*, 1261–72 in Whitbeck), *Brihtrīc* (*Brictrice flat*, c. 1180 in Scaleby), *Brihtwine* (Brightenflat), *Brūnhelm* (Brownelson), *Cospatric*, from *Gwæspatric* (see 508), **Deall* (Dalston), *Dudd* (Duddon (?)), *Dunning* (Dunningwell), *Eadgȳð* (f) (*Editheknot*), *Ēadmund* (*Edmundecrok'*, 1371 in Penrith), *Ēadrīc* (*Edrikescroft*, 1180–1210 in Whitbeck), *Ēadwulf* (*Castelyadolfbek*, 1278 in Threlkeld), *Ēanbald* (Embleton (?)), *Ecci* (this or *Ecgi* is suggested by the earliest forms for Easby: the other forms suggest *Ese*), **Ecgel* (Eaglesfield), **Frisa* (Frizington), *Gōdrīc* (Gutherscale, Gutterby (2), *Godrik-how*, 1479 in Renwick), *Gūðbeorht* (*Godbrigholm*, c. 1280 in Above Derwent), **Hæfer* (Harrington), **Hudd* (Huddlesceugh), *Hwīta* (Whicham, Cumwhitton), **Isa* (Isel), *Lēofhere* (Laversdale),

Lēofrīc (*Levericpule*, c. 1235 in Bootle), *Lēofwine* (*Lewinebrigg*, c. 1210 in Westlinton), *Oswald* (Birdoswald), **Perd*(*i*) (Pardshaw), **Rōta* (Rottington), *Sǣburh* (f) (Sebergham (?)), *Tūnwine* (*Tonewinekelde*, c. 1210 in Brampton), *Ūhtrēd* (Oughterby, Oughterside), **Weorc*, **Wyrc* (Workington), *Wicga* (Wigton), **Wulfa* (Oulton).

(b) Scandinavian

Afaster (OSw, a personal name corresponding to this is probably the first element of Austhwaite), *Anund* (*Ananderdale*, earlier name of Ennerdale), *Armi* (Armboth (?)), *Arni* (*Arneshowe* and possibly *Arneraid*, 1209–10 in Borrowdale), *Arnolf* (Arnaby), *Ásgeirr* (Askerton), *Ave* (ODan) (Aiglegill), *Barni* (ODan) (Barn Scar), *Bǫrkr* (*Barkerhals*, 1300 in Millom), *Brandr* (*Brandesdic*, c. 1180 in Flimby), *Brynhildr* (f) (*Brundeshole, Brunildhole*, 1261 in Rottington), *Einarr* (Annaside), *Finnþórr* (*Gillefinchor*), *Fólki* (*Folkegile*, c. 1174 in Flimby), *Forni* (Fornside, Thornby (?)), *Setforn'*, c. 1215 in Muncaster), *Fróði* (Feather Knott), *Gamall* (Gamblesby, Gamelsby, *Gamelsheued*, 1272 in Hesket in the Forest, *Gamelesflat*, 1274 in Skirwith), *Grennir* (OWScand) (Grinsdale (?)), *Grímr* (*Grymesholme*, 1371 in Great Salkeld), *Gunnar* (*Tarngunerigg*, 1725 in Workington), *Halfdan* (Alston), *Hermundr* (Armaside (?)), *Hlóra* (f) (Lorton, the name may be that of a stream, not a person), *Hrafn* (*Rauenesgil*, Ravensgill Plantation, Renwick), *Hróþulfr* (Hutton Roof (?)), **Húkmaðr* (Upmanby), *Húni* (Honister Crag (?)), *Ingiríðr* (f) (*Ingrehowe*, 1410 in Cleator), *Kárr* (Kersey Bridge (?)), *Ketil* (Keskadale, *Ketelscalerbech, Ketescalrig*, c. 1220 in Under Skiddaw), *Kolli* (Coledale (?)), **Krakande* (*Craconflat*, 1338 in Egremont (?)), *Kráki* (Cracrop (?)), *Langlíf* (f) (Langley), *Leggr* (Legburthwaite), *Máni* (Dalemain), *Mōthir* (ODan) (Motherby), *Múli* (Muncaster (?)), *Músi* (Mousthwaite Comb (?)), *Nate* (Nattrass (?)), *Óli* (*Olebec*, 1195 in Embleton), *Ormr* (Hornsby, *Ormesby, Ormescroft*, c. 1265 in Setmurthy, 1542 in Bootle), *Orri* (Orton, Over Water (?)), *Palmi* (*Palme Castell* (?)), *Sigmundr* (Simon Kell, Simonscales; alternatively both names might contain OE *Sigemund*, but this is less likely), *Sigríðr* (f) (Sillathwaite (?), *Sighrethcroft*, no date in Caldbeck, *Sirithlandes*, 1338 in Egremont), *Sigvarðr* (*Sywardekelde*, c. 1210 in Brampton), *Skalli* (Scawthwaite Close, *Scalleflat*, 1245 in Edenhall), *Skjǫldr* (Scalderscew), *Snarri* (Snary Beck)[1], *Súle* (ODan) (Soulby), a weak feminine name corresponding to the strong masculine *Sundvíss* occurs in *cruce Sundwize*, 1195 in Embleton, *Sunnifa* (f) (Sunnygill Beck), *Sveinn* (*Suanesate*, c. 1174 in Flimby), *Þorbrand* (*Thorbrancroft* c. 1250 in Edenhall), *Þorfin* (*Briggethorfin, Thorfinesakyr* c. 1210 in Tallentire),

---

[1] *Sǫð* (f) possibly occurs in *Satberton*.

Þóri or Þúri (Thursby), Þorkell (*Thurkilhou*, 1245 in Edenhall), Þorsteinn (Thurstonfield), Þór(v)aldr (*Thoroldwath*), Þyrne (*Thirneby* (?)), Tósti (*Tostihow*), Úlfr (Ousby, Uldale (?), Ullswater, *Lakewolf*, Ulnescarthbec, c. 1203 in Mosser, Ulvescroft, c. 1212 in Ponsonby, *vlueshouse*, 1276 in Wythop), Úlfkell (Brotherilkeld), Úri (*Ureby Field* (?)), Úspakr (Keldhouse Bridge).

Dufa or Dufe, which occurs somewhat frequently in early documents from the Danelaw, and is the first element of Dowthwaitehead, may represent either the ON feminine name *Dúfa* or an unrecorded English equivalent.

(c) ANGLO-SCANDINAVIAN

Arnketell (Arkleby, *Arkylcroft*, c. 1265 in Setmurthy, *Arkelflat* c. 1260 in Tallentire), Asten (Alstonby, *Astinhole*, 1261 in Rottington), Dolfin (Dolphenby), Faremann (Farmanby), Ouþen (*Houthenhou, Houthunhou*, c. 1240 in Gosforth), Walþéof (*Waldeylond*, 1338 in Dean).

(d) MIDDLE ENGLISH AND CONTINENTAL

Adam (Adamgill Head), Agyllun (Norman French) (Aglionby), Ainulf (representing OGer *Aginulf, Einolf*, a continental name current in England before the Norman Conquest) (*Aynolfebergh'*, c. 1285 in Oulton), Alein (French, of Breton origin) (Allonby, Ellonby, Starling Dodd), Anneis (f, colloquial form of *Agnes*) (*Anneislandes*, 1338 in Egremont), Austin (*Austineflat*, c. 1230 in Dundraw), Aymer (grangia Haymeri, c. 1202 in Ponsonby), Baldwin (Baldwinholme), Bastun (Anglo-French) (Bassenthwaite, Bassenthwaite Lake), Benet (*Stibenet*, 1278 in Threlkeld), Bernard (French) (*Bernardhou*, c. 1250 in Rottington), Blundel, Blondel (French) (Blunderfield), Bochard (French form of OGer *Burchard*) (Botcherby, Botchergate), Bret (*Brezhou*, c. 1250 in Rottington), David (Davygill), Dormond (Dormansteads), Etard (French, of German origin) (Etterby), Francis[1] (*Frauncishowes*, 1338 in Egremont), Fulk (*Fulkeholme*, 1589 in St Cuthbert Without), Gerard (Continental-Germanic) (Garrigill), Godard (Norman form of OGer *Godehard*) (Godderthwaite (?), Satgodard), Godfrey (*Godefraicroft*, a. 1240 in Burgh by Sands), Grewcock (*Grucokgille*, a. 1225 in Gosforth), Grimbald (Continental-Germanic) (*Grimbaldhenge*, c. 1340–50 in Carlisle), Gumer (*Gumerholm*, late 13th century in Gosforth), Henry (French) (Harraby, Henryholm, 15th century in Warwick), Herlewin (ME, from OFr *Herluin*) (*Helewynherge*, c. 1230 in Gosforth (?)), Hubert (Continental-Germanic) (Knockupworth, Upperby), Humphrey (English form of French *Onfroi*, from OGer *Hunfrid*) (Humphrie's Ho), Ibbet

---

[1] The name did not become common in England till the 16th century but may have been in use earlier as a Christian name, not just as a nickname.

(f, diminutive of Isabel) (*Burntippet Moor* (?)), *Isaac* (*Isaacby*), *John* (Johnby, Hutton John), *Kyttoc* (f, diminutive of Catharine) (*Peyekyttoc*, c. 1165 in Grinsdale (?)), *Lambert* (Lamperthills), *Lambin* (a ME short form of the preceding name) (Lamonby), *Mabel* (f) (Mabil Cross), *Martin* (Martin Tarn), *Maurice* (French) (Moresby), *Ne(a)le* (Nealhouse, *Nelesbigginge*), *Nevin* (*Nevincroft*, c. 1235 in Ellenborough), *Nicholas* (Nicholforest), *Puncun* (French) (Ponsonby), *Quintin* (brought to England by the Normans and used not infrequently in pre-reformation Scotland) (Cumwhinton), *Rainald* (*Raynaldclose*, 1391 in Hesket in the Forest), *Randolf* (Norman, from Norse *Randulfr*) (Randalholm Hall, Randalinton, *Randerside Hall*, *Randulusat*, t. Hy 3 in Sebergham), *Rauf* (modern Ralph) (*Raufbrig'*, c. 1340–50 in Dalston), *Rayner* (brought to England by the Normans, derived from OGer *Raganher*) (*Raynersete*, 1363 in Burgh by Sands), *Ricard* (French) (Rickerby, Rickergate, *Ricarsit*, 1303 in Ellenborough, *Richardecroft*, 1338 in Egremont), *Robert* (French) (Robberby, *Robertaker*, 1332 in Boltons), *Roger* (French) (Rogerscale, Rogersceugh, *Rogerside*, *Rogerpot*, 1303 in Ellenborough), *Scot(h)ard* (OGer) (Skitby), *Susan* (f) (*fontem Susanne*, c. 1210 in Embleton), *Terri* (OFr, a derivative of OGer *Theodoric*, *Theuderich*) (Tarraby), *Walter* (*Walterlandes*, c. 1290 in Dalston), *Werri* (Willow Holme), *Wigan* (OFr, of Breton origin) (Wiggonby), *William* (*Williamfeld*, 1363 in Egremont), *Wilmer* or *Winmer* (Wormanby (?)), *Wygar* (Wickerthwaite: the name might be ON *Vigarr*).

(e) GOIDELIC

Branán (*Stanbrenan*), *Brandán* (*Fitbrandan*), *Bueth* (Boothby), *Cambán* (Gillcambon), *Cartán* (Hobcartan), *Colmán* (*Watchcomon*), *Corc* (Corby and *Korkgill*, 1542 in Muncaster), *Corcán* (Mockerkin), *Crín* (*Croscrin*, c. 1200 in Kirkoswald), *Cros(s)án* (*Kirkeby Crossan*), *Donald* (from Gaelic *Domhnall*) (*Donald-crofte*, 1479 in Renwick), *Dufan* (from OIr *Dubhán*) (Dovenby), *Dungal* (*Thueitdounegaleg'*), **Gearrán* (Gilgarran (?)), *Gillamáirtin* (*Gill martyne ridding*, t. John in Thursby), *Gillamicháil* (*Gillemihelecroft*, c. 1205 in Whicham, and *Gillenukelstagge* (*sic*), c. 1260 in Under Skiddaw), *Gille* (Gilsland and *Gillecroft*, c. 1205 in Whicham), *Glas* (Ravenglass), *Glas(s)án* (Glassonby), **Lennóc* (*Staynlenok*), *Linán* (Drumleaning), *Lochán* (Laconby (?)), *Mabanán*, *Mobanán* (Setmabanning), *Macóg* (*Skalmallock* (?)), *Maenach* (Scarrowmanwick (?)), *Melmor* (from OIr *Maelmuire*) (Melmerby), *Mungo* (Mungrisdale (?) and *Mungowcroft'*, c. 1340–50 in Dalston), *Murdoch* (from OIr *Muiredach*) (Setmurthy and *Karcmurdath*, c. 1200 in Hayton), *Patric* (Aspatria and *Patrikles*, 1450 in Kirkbampton), *Suthán* (Greysouthen), *Ternan* (*Polterternan*).

For further information about these names, *v.* Introduction, pp. xxiii–xxv.

(*f*) BRITISH AND OLD WELSH

Danoc (*Caer-Thannock*, later styled Maidencastle), *Dinoot* (Cardunneth Pike (?)), **Dubācos* (Cumdivock, Devoke Water: in the latter case the name might be that of the lake, not of a person), *Dunmail* (Dunmail Raise), *Ewein* (Castle Hewin), *Guencat* (a British name corresponding to this OWelsh one is the second element of *Couwhencatte*), *Gwaspatric*, anglicised as *Gospatric* or *Cospatric*, (*Waspatrickwath, Cospatricseye*, 1169 in Walton), *Gwenddoleu* (Carwinley (?)), *Gwyddelan* (Tarn Wadling), *Merchiaun* (Pow Maughan, Maughonby), *Meriaun* (Marron (?), *Tarn Marron* (?)), *Teiliau* (Carnetley), *Troite* (bek *Troyte*).

APPENDIX: ROMANO-BRITISH NAMES
IN CUMBERLAND

THE SOURCES OF FORMS

ANTONINE ITIN. *Itineraria Antonini Augusti et Burdigalense (Itineraria Romana I*), ed. O. Cuntz, Leipzig 1929.

INSCRIPTIONS (Chesters) *An Account of the Roman Antiquities preserved in the Museum at Chesters, Northumberland*, Second Edition, London 1907.

INSCRIPTIONS (7/...) *Corpus Inscriptionum Latinarum* vii, ed. AEmilius Hübner, Berlin 1873 (cited by number, not page).

INSCRIPTIONS (Rudge) J. D. Cowan and I. A. Richmond, "The Rudge Cup" (*Archæologia Æliana*, Fourth Series, xii, 310–42).

NOTITIA *Notitia Dignitatum*, ed. O. Seeck, Berlin 1876.

PTOLEMY *Claudii Ptolemæi Geographia*, ed. Carolus Mullerus [Karl Müller], Paris 1883–1901.

RAVENNAS *Ravennatis Anonymi Cosmographia et Guidonis Geographica (Itineraria Romana II*), ed. J. Schnetz, Leipzig 1940.

IDENTIFICATION AND INTERPRETATION

J. Collingwood Bruce, *Handbook to the Roman Wall*, Tenth Edition, ed. I. A. Richmond, Newcastle-upon-Tyne 1947.

K. Jackson, "On some Romano-British Place-Names" (*Journal of Roman Studies* xxxviii, 54–8).

A. Longnon, *Les Noms de Lieu de la France*, Paris 1920–9.

I. A. Richmond and O. G. S. Crawford, "The British Section of the Ravenna Cosmography" (*Archaeologia* xciii, 1–50, cited as *Arch.*).

NOTES ON ROMANO-BRITISH NAMES
IN CUMBERLAND

ABALLAVA. Cf. W *afall* 'appletree' (*Arch.* 23–4).

ALAVNA, originally the name of the R. Ellen. Cf. Ptolemy's Ἀλαῦνα = Alnwick Nb, W *Alun* (< OCelt **Alaun*-), an epithet applied to rivers and gods and men (*Arch.* 22).

BANNA. Cf. W, Breton, *ban* 'peak, horn,' and *Bannovalum* (also in Ravennas) = Caister L (*Arch.* 24).

[*continued on p.* 512

ROMANO-BRITISH

IDENTIFICATION	ANTONINE ITIN.	NOTITIA
Birdoswald 115		*Amboglanna*
Bewcastle 60		
Castlesteads 114		*Axeloduno*
Netherby 53	*Castra Exploratorum*	
Stanwix 108		*Petrianis*
Carlisle 40	*Luguvallo*	*Lagubalio*
	Luguvalio	
?		*Congavata*
?		
Burgh by Sands 126		*Aballaba*
Bowness 123		
Beckfoot 295		
Ellenborough 284		*Alauna*
Moresby 421		*Gabrosenti*
St Bees Head 430		*Tunnocelo*
Ravenglass 425	*Clanoventa*	*Glannibanta*
Hard Knott 343		
Papcastle 308		
?Old Carlisle 330		
Old Penrith 235	*Voreda*	
R. Eden 12	Ἰτούνα (Ptolemy)	

NAMES IN CUMBERLAND

RAVENNAS	INSCRIPTIONS	NORMALISED
Gabaglanda	CAMBOGLANS (Rudge)	CAMBOGLANNA
Banna	BANNA (Rudge); VENATORES BANNIENSES (7/830)	BANNA
Uxelludamo	VXELODVM (Rudge)	VXELLODVNVM
		CASTRA EX-PLORATORUM
	AL · PETR. (7/323); AL · PET. (7/872); PRAEF · ALAE AVGVSTAE PETR-IANAE TORQ. (7/929); A PET · (Chesters, No. 258)	PETRIANAE
Lagubal(i)um		LVGVVALIVM
		CONGAVATA
Fanocodi		FANVM COCIDI
Avalana	ABALLAVA (Rudge); FRISIONVM ABALLAVENSIVM (7/415)	ABALLAVA
Maio, Maia	MAIS (Rudge)	MAIA
Bribra		? BIBRA
Alauna		ALAVNA
Gabrocentio		GABROSENTVM
Iuliocenon		? ITVNOCELVM
Cantiventi		CLANOVENTA
Medibogdo		?
Derventione		DERVENTIO
Olerica		?
Bereda		VEREDA or VOREDA
		ITVNA

(?) BIBRA. Cf. perhaps the first element of *Bebronna* (*Bibronna*) 'spring of the beavers' (Longnon, p. 54). Here it may mean 'brown (river).'

CAMBOGLANNA. Cf. W *cam* (OBrit *cambo-*, as in *Camboritum*) 'crooked' and *glann* 'bank' (*Arch.* 34). See also K. Jackson (*Modern Philology* xciii, 56), who points out that O. G. S. Crawford's identification of Arthur's battle at *Camlann* with *Camboglanna* is philologically perfectly possible, though whether the identification is certain enough on other grounds to be canonised in the *Map of Britain in the Dark Ages* is perhaps a different question.

CASTRA EXPLORATORVM, 'fort of the Scouts' (see *supra* 53).

CLANOVENTA. Cf. W *glann* 'bank, shore' (JRS xxxviii, 55–6), and -*went* 'place, field' (*Arch.* 27).

CONGAVATA. ?.

DERVENTIO, originally the name of the R. Derwent. Cf. W *derw* 'oak'+suffix -*ydd* (*Arch.* 31; AA⁴ xii, 339).

FANVM COCIDI, 'shrine of Cocidius' (perhaps a derivative of OBrit *cocco-*, W *coch*, 'red'), a god worshipped especially in the triangle between Bewcastle, Netherby and Stanwix (*Arch.* 34).

GABROSENTVM. Cf. W *gafr* 'he-goat' and *hynt* (OIrish *sēt*, Breton *hent*) 'path' (*Arch.* 35).

ITVNA, the R. Eden (see *supra* 12).

(?) ITVNOCELVM, 'Eden Headland', conceivably a lost site near Egremont [I.A.R.]. Cf. OBrit **ocelon* 'promontory' (*Arch.* 36).

LVGVVALIVM, 'place of Luguvalos' (see *supra* 40–2).

MAIA, ? 'the larger.' Cf. W *mwy* from OBrit **māios*, comparative of **māros* (*Arch.* 38).

MEDIBOGDO, ? 'in the middle of the curve' (*Arch.* 40).

OLERICA, ? cf. W *alarch* 'swan' (*Arch.* 42–3).

PETRIANAE gets its name from the *Ala Petriana*, a Gallic unit of auxiliary horse, long stationed on the Wall (JRS xxi, 130).

VXELLODVNVM. Cf. *Uxellodunum*, probably to be identified with the Puy d'Issolu near Vayrac (Dept. Lot), and W *uchel* and *din*, hence 'high stronghold' (*Arch.* 47–8).

VEREDA or VOREDA. ? Cf. Gaulish *ue-* (as in Latin *uesper*, *uescor*) or OW *guo-*, and W *rhwydd* 'easy, free from obstruction' (*Arch.* 24–5).[1]

[1] We are much indebted to Professor I. A. Richmond for his help in dealing with these problems.

LIST

OF SOME WORDS OF WHICH THE HISTORY
IS ILLUSTRATED IN THESE VOLUMES

INDEX

OF PLACE-NAMES IN CUMBERLAND

Where a place-name is mentioned on several pages, the primary reference or references are given first in clarendon figures. Field-names have not in general been indexed (except for those which are discussed in the Introduction) but all other names are included. In Part III, the Introduction, the Addenda etc., to Vols. XX and XXI and the Appendix on Romano-British names have been indexed, but not the Notes on the Dialect or the Lists of Elements.

[1] *v.* also list of elements, p. 469.

[1] *v.* also list of elements, p. 469.

Shepherds Crag, 353
Shield, 129
Shieldside Wood, 193
Shield Water, 26
Shivery Knott, 353
Shopford, 58
Shortdale, 111
Short Shank, 64
Shotfoot, 98
Shoulthwaite, Shoulthwaite Moss, 314
Show Burn, 27
Shundraw, 314
Sickergill, 250
Side, 340
Side Fell, 58
Sike, 258
Sikebeck, 348
Sikeside, 91
Sike Whins, 400
Silecroft, 444–5
Sillathwaite, 387
Sillerea Wood, 225, 121
Silloth, 293–4
Sillyhall, High and Low, 179
Silver Beck, 27
Silver Cove, 386
Silver Hill, 373
Silver How, 396
Silver Side and Top, 86
Simon Kell, 386
Simonscales, 363
Simon's Onset, 106
Sinen Gill, 35
Siney Tarn, 35
Sinks Beck, 292
Skalmallok, 269, xxiv, xxv
Skelda, 347
Skelgill (in Above Derwent), 371, 381
Skelgill, High, Low and Middle (in Alston), 179
Skellerah, 365
Skelling, 243, 217
Skelling Moor, 217
Skelly Neb, 258
Skelsceugh, 337
Skelton, Skelton Pasture, Skelton Wood End, 239–40
Skiddaw, Skiddaw Forest and Man, 319–20
Skill Beck, 27, xix
Skinburness, 294
Skiprigg, 135

Skirsgill, 189
Skirting Beck, 4
Skirwith, Skirwith Abbey, Fell and Hall, 242–3
Skitby, 103
Skitter Beck (now Bitter Beck), 4
Skitwath Beck, 27
Skydes, 179
Slack (in Ainstable), 170
   (in Westward), 331
Slackhead, 93
Slack Ho, 117
Slacks, 64
Slaggie Burn, 27
Slaggieburn, 179
Slapestone, 419
Slapestones, 404
Slates Cleugh, 179
Sleathwaite, 404
Sledbank, 445–6
Sleet Beck, 27
Sleightholme, 292
Slight Side, 392
Slittery Ford, 117
Smaithwaite (in St John's), Smaithwaite Bridge, 314–15
Smaithwaite (in Lamplugh), 407
Smallthwaite, 419
Smallthwaite Ho, 242
Smalmstown, 99
Smithsteads (in Askerton), 58
   (in Solport), 108
Smithybanks Wood, 368
Smithy Beck, 27, xxxviii
Smithy Ho, 317
Snab (in Caldbeck), 279
Snab, High and Low (in Above Derwent), 373
Snab End, 179
Snab Murris, 367, xxiv
Snappergill, 179
Snary Beck and Bridge, 27, xxiii
Sneckgate, 379
Sneckyeat Plantation, 379
Snellings, 381
Snipes How, 317
Snittlegarth, 265
Snowden Close, 116
Sokbrodland, 278
Solmain, 115
Solport, Solport Mill, 107, xx n.
Solum, 40
Solway Firth, Moss and Sands, 39–40

INDEX

OF PLACE-NAMES IN COUNTIES OTHER THAN
CUMBERLAND

[A few foreign place-names referred to in the text have
been included in this Index.]

LIST OF PARISHES AS KEY TO MAP

ESKDALE WARD

1 Arthuret
2 Askerton
[3 Bellbank, to 30]
4 Bewcastle
5 Brampton
6 Burtholme
7 Carlatton
8+15 Castle Carrock
[9 Crosby-on-Eden, to E 29 and C20]
10 Cumrew [+part of L 6, −part to L 1]
11 Cumwhitton
12 Upper Denton
13 Nether Denton
14 Farlam
[15 Geltsdale, to 8]
16 Hayton
17 Hethersgill
18 Irthington
19 Kingmoor
20 Kingwater
21, 22, 23 Kirkandrews
24 Kirklinton Middle
25 Midgeholme
26 Nicholforest
27 Scaleby
28+31 Solport
29 Stanwix [+part of E 9, −part to C 20]
30+3 Stapleton
[31 Trough, to 28]
32 Walton
33 Waterhead
34 Westlinton

CUMBERLAND WARD

1 Aikton
2+9, 10 Beaumont
[3 Blencogo, to B 11]
4 Bowness
5 Burgh by Sands
6 Cummersdale
7 Dalston
8 Dundraw
[9 Grinsdale, to 2]
[10 Kirkandrews upon Eden, to 2]
11 Kirkbampton
12 Kirkbride
13 Orton
14 Rockcliffe

15+22 St Cuthbert Without
16+part of L 36 Sebergham
17 Thursby
[18 Warwick, to 20]
19 Waverton
20 Wetheral [+ 18 and parts of E 9 and of E 29]
21 Wigton
[22 Wreay, to 15]

LEATH WARD

1 Ainstable + parts of 6 and E 10
2 Alston
[3 Berrier and Murrah, to 26]
[4 Bowscale, to 26]
5+27 Catterlen
[6 Croglin, to 1 and E 10]
7+19, 35 Culgaith
8 Dacre
[9 Edenhall, to 21]
[10 Gamblesby, to 11]
11+10 Glassonby
12 Greystoke
13+30 Hesket [in the Forest]
14+33 Hunsonby and Winskill
[15 Hutton-in-the-Forest, to 34]
16+18 Hutton [John and Soil]
[17 Hutton Roof, to 26]
[18 Hutton Soil, united with Hutton John]
[19 Kirkland and Blencarn, to 7]
20+31, 37 Kirkoswald
21+9 Langwathby
22 Lazonby
23+39 Matterdale
[24 Melmerby, to 28]
[25 Middlesceugh and Braithwaite, to 34]
26+3, 4, 17, B 32 Mungrisdale
[27 Newton Reigny, to 5]
28+24 Ousby
29 Penrith
[30 Plumpton Wall, to 13]
[31 Renwick, to 20]
32 Great Salkeld
[33 Little Salkeld, to 14]
34+15, 25 Skelton
[35 Skirwith, to 7]
36 Castle Sowerby [−part to C 16]
[37 Staffield, to 20]
38 Threlkeld
[39 Watermillock, to 23]

ALLERDALE BELOW
DERWENT WARD

1 Allhallows
2 Allonby
3 Aspatria
4 Bassenthwaite
5 Bewaldeth
6+45 Blennerhasset and Kirkland
7+29, 43 Blindcrake, Isel and Redmain
8 Boltons
9 Bothel and Threapland
10+18, 44 Bridekirk
11+31, C 3 Bromfield
12 Broughton
13 Broughton Moor
14 Caldbeck
15+38 Camerton
16 Crosscanonby
17 Dearham
[18 Dovenby, to 10]
19 Ellenborough and Ewanrigg, amalgamated with 33 to form the parish of Maryport
[20 Flimby, added to Maryport]
21 Gilcrux
22 Hayton and Mealo
23 Holme Abbey
24 Holme East Waver
25 Holme Low
26 Holme St Cuthbert
27, 28 Ireby
[29 Isel Old Park, to 7]
30 Keswick
[31 Langrigg and Mealrigg, to 11]
[32 Mosedale, to L 26]
[33 Netherhall, amalgamated with 19]
34 Oughterside and Allerby
[35 Oulton, to 49]
36 Papcastle [−part to A 15]
37 Plumbland
[38 Ribton, to 15]
39 St John's, Castlerigg and Wythburn
40 Seaton
[41 Skiddaw, to 42]
42+41 Underskiddaw
[43 Sunderland, to 7]
[44 Tallentire, to 10]
[45 Torpenhow, to 6]
[46 Uldale, to 27, 28]
47 Westnewton
48 Westward
49+35 Woodside

ALLERDALE ABOVE
DERWENT WARD

1 Arlecdon
2+part of 28 St Bridget Beckermet
3+part of 35 St John Beckermet

[4 Birker and Austhwaite, to 25]
5+38, 55 Blindbothel
6 Bootle
7 Borrowdale
[8 Brackenthwaite, to 10
9 Brigham
10+8 Buttermere
11 Cleator
12 Great Clifton
13 Little Clifton
[14 Cloffocks, to 59]
15 Cockermouth [+part of B 36, −part to 48]
[16 Corney, to 51]
17+21 Dean
18 Above Derwent
19 Distington
20 Drigg and Carleton
[21 Eaglesfield, to 17]
22 Egremont
23 Embleton
24 Ennerdale and Kinniside
25+4 Eskdale and Wasdale [−part to 52]
26 Gosforth
27 Greysouthen
28 Haile [−part to 2]
29 Harrington (now Lowca) [−part to 59]
[30 Hensingham, to 44, 53, 57]
31+part of 52 Irton with Santon
32+45 Lamplugh
33 Lorton
34 Loweswater
35 Lowside Quarter [−part to 3]
36 Millom
37 Moresby [−part to 57]
[38 Mosser, to 5]
39 Muncaster
40 Parton
41 Ponsonby
[42 Preston Quarter, to 43, 57]
43+parts of 42, 46 Rottington
44+part of 30 St Bees
[45 Salter, to 32]
[46 Sandwith, to 43, 57]
47 Seascale
48+part of 15 Setmurthy
[49 Stainburn, to 58, 59]
50 Ulpha
51+16 Waberthwaite
52 Nether Wasdale [+part of 25, −part to 31]
53+part of 30 Weddicar
54+56 Whicham
[55 Whinfell, to 5]
[56 Whitbeck, to 54]
57+parts of 30, 37, 42, 46 Whitehaven
58+part of 49 Winscales
59+14 and parts of 29, 49 Workington
60 Wythop